AS IT WAS IN THE BEGINNING

VOLUME TWO

EWURAMMA

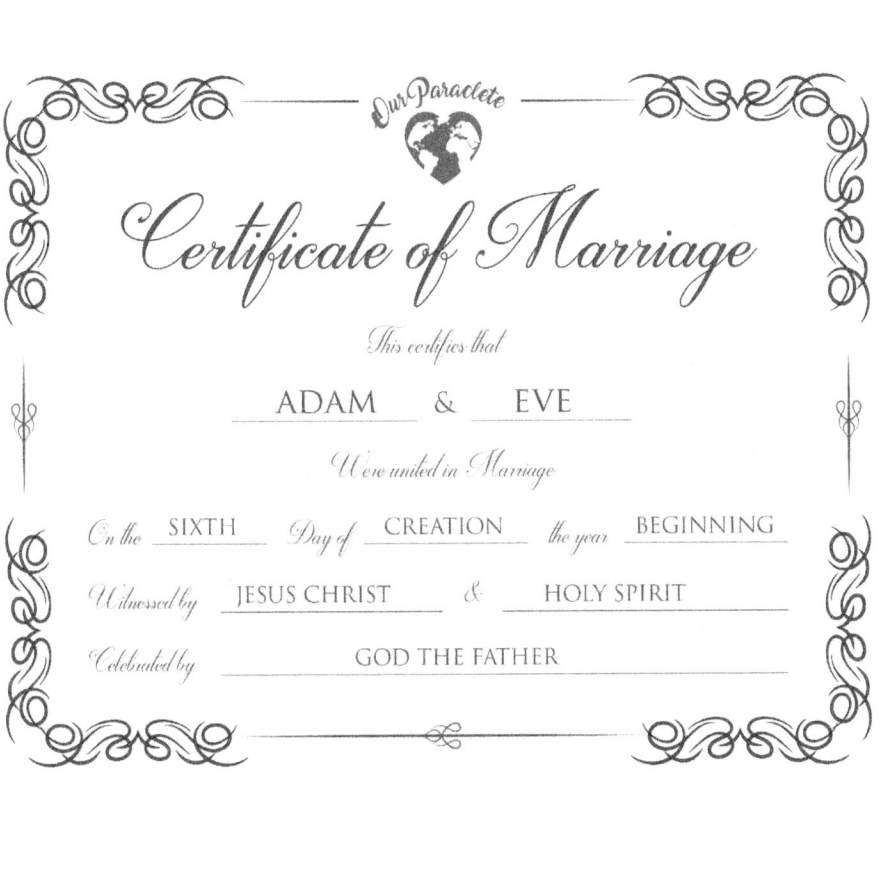

AS IT WAS IN THE BEGINNING

Copyright © 2023 by Ewuramma
All rights reserved.

ISBN: 978-1-524763-1-3
E-Book ISBN: 978-1-524763-1-5

Copyright © 2023 Our Paraclete. All rights reserved.
Published by: Our Paraclete, an imprint of Our Paraclete Publishers.

All rights reserved. No part of this book may be reproduced or transmitted in any form or by any means, electronic or mechanical, including photocopying, recording, or by any information storage and retrieval system, without permission in writing from the publisher.

Unless otherwise indicated, all Scriptures are taken from the Holy Bible, Amplified Bible, Classic Edition®, AMPC®. Copyright © 1962, 1964, 1965, 1987 by Biblica, Inc.™, used by permission of Zondervan. All rights reserved worldwide. www.zondervan.com. The "NIV" and "New International Version" are trademarks registered in the United States Patent and Trademark Office by Biblica, Inc.

Contact Author on:

ourparacletefoundation.inc@gmail.com

Design & Print by:

Indes Procom Ltd.
www.indesprocom.com

Cover Credit:

Richard Opoku Agyeman
Director, Acute Formula

CONTENTS OF VOL. II

Dedication	*vi*
Apologia	*ix*
Foreword	*xiii*
Endorsements	*xviii*

CHAPTER 01
Marriage Is A Gift — *01*

CHAPTER 02
The Actual Marriage Race — *15*

CHAPTER 03
Everyone Deserves Love — *22*

CHAPTER 04
"Conversion" of The Man's Love And The Woman's Submission — *31*

CHAPTER 05
The Faithful Husband In An Unfaithful Marriage — *53*

CHAPTER 06
The Mystery of Divorce — *65*

CHAPTER 07
Compassion For The Ignorant — *125*

CHAPTER 08
Singlehood Must Not Be Seen As Ungodly — *139*

CHAPTER 09
The Flesh Dishonors Marriage — *159*

CHAPTER 10
Wasted Hours In Promisquity — *177*

CHAPTER 11
Marriage Is A Celebration of The Bride And The Groom — *189*

DEDICATION

I dedicate the book to the man who was my elder, father and friend,
Elder Thomas Godfrey Kofi Gyampoh

"In the year when king Uzziah died I saw also the Lord sitting upon a throne, high and lifted up, and his train filled the temple." Isaiah 6:1

Before anyone knew I could do anything in the house of God in the United States, you told me what I had not seen. In my girlhood, while I was yet a stripling, you persuaded me to be an adult Christian and play the woman for God of my fathers and mothers.

No one can ever overestimate the great privilege God has given me through your help and nurture in God. In my girlhood mind, I did not understand why you assigned me to lead worship every time the then national Head Apostle Alex Osei Bonsu and the then New York District pastor Overseer Andrew Kwabena Donkor visited our assembly (Queens). As it's typical of me, I approached you but asked a seemingly negative question. "Elder, why do you want to drive me away from the church?" You laughed and calmly said: "No, God has deposited something in you, and I want to help you."

You loved the Lord who has called you to Himself so very much; hence, you loved everyone and everything that promoted His course. We all were not able, as yet, to bear the full revelation of Providence when He permitted me to be taken away from you and Mama Vida's guardianship. But Our Lord Jesus possessed the wisdom to understand it all.

Satan did everything to have made me forget the God of my fathers. Everywhere around me, I saw sorrow and heartache. I had so much to tell you every time I saw you, but I became dumb for over a decade.

On that fateful day when you persuaded me to talk, you did something that is not often said about African men. You wept. Your tears were a very Instructive fact to me. It was full of consolation to tell me that someone cared about me. You are a man yet with a woman's heart. Anyone who knows can never doubt how strict and principled you were. Yet as a man, you lived, related, and cared as a Mother HEN covering everyone that crossed paths with you with your wings. Oh, how I wish you could hear me say that I will arise by the grace of God. I will become everything you saw God could make me become.

I am also sure God that I will not only be a specimen of a tried Christian but also of a specimen of a graced Christian. And God will surely be praised for every moment of my life. When you bowed your head to death, it, in fact, reminded a new me of the origin of my commission— Go ye, therefore, and teach all nations (Mark 16:15). Having life and motion, I will use my pain-turned-power with prudence and discretion. My biography will never end with the false triumph of the devil over me.

There is no word capable of conveying all that I mean to say. But I want to assure you that by the Word of our Lord Jesus and by His Spirit, I mean to win the victory. By the testimony of a weak and feeble me to the gospel of Jesus' grace, I mean to conquer the powers of darkness.

I thank you and Mama Vida and all the children for everything. May your gentle and selfless soul continue to rest in the bosom of our Lord and Savior, Jesus Christ.

— Ewuramma

Apologia

Most people I know, who marry, hope their relationship will be like Romeo and Juliet's if not the Titanic love story. And while many of them see their dreams come true, many other promising marriages struggle, and others, unfortunately, end in divorce.

What's the trick? Is it just that those who enjoy their marriages and stay married know better how to choose their life partners than those who do not? Of course, many reasons could be offered; at the very least, many justifications could be revised. My thoughts on the subject are as follows: A married relationship is the consequence of *faith* and *love*. Thus, it takes absolute faith and love for two finite people to entrust the rest of their lives and their children's to someone they cannot know who and what they will become in the next 10 seconds. Nevertheless, it is faith that motivates them to make such a courageous move. And whenever and wherever faith sets out to achieve something, she is joined by love.

Although many people believe that any man or any woman makes a good husband or a good wife, I respectfully disagree. A godly and loyal man or woman who seeks an everlasting relationship seeks a spouse who is like them in character and preference. A survey study of over 10,000 people looking for marriage partners discovered that kindness was "universally sought". While a man seeks a kindhearted wife, a woman seeks someone with a matching disposition. In a broad sense, a kindhearted person is a loyal person. They are selfless and have the grace and capacity to build friendships and empathy when it comes to parenting children.

Marriage is also a choice, and most people consider it to be an enlightening and happy experience. Regardless of how two people enter a marriage, whether, by choice or arrangement, it is not legitimate until there is a choice on both sides to make the marriage work. Couples who are compelled into marriages in cultures that still recognize arranged marriages do not abandon the marriage even if they are initially very dissatisfied. They do not end the relationship and move on with their lives. Instead, by sticking together, they make it work.

Choice of marriage and choice in the marriage must be mutual. It implies that both sides should have a blessed choice to make it a true marriage.

It is unhealthy when there is a stark contrast between a husband and a wife; when one is on the extreme left and the other on the far right. In such a home, no matter how much God may bless the family in all other respects, there will be a great miss in it. Like the eclipsed sun, that part of family life that should be all light will be left in thick darkness.

A very similar analogy is the American election of a president and vice president in 2020. It serves in both roles to the great benefit of depicting a home and how the human race began in the Garden of Eden. The then former Vice President Joseph Robinette Biden, the Democratic presidential nominee at the time, was like an eligible bachelor. President Joseph R. Biden, like Adam, required a helpmate to assist him in managing his household (America) and parenting his children (American citizens). Thus, he had absolute power over the significant person he chose to label "Vice President" in his cabinet. That is when faith emerges as an unavoidable virtue.

Apologia

In his very delicate audition for a vice presidential selection, President Joseph Biden, like an eligible bachelor with all the women at his disposal to choose from, had Senator Harris and four others - Senator Elizabeth Warren, Governor Gretchen Whitmer, and Susan E. Rice at his disposal. Just as a man's choice of a woman significantly impacts his life, any decision Mr. Biden made had a significant impact on his victory in the 2020 general election.

"It may be the most important decision they make or at least, one of the most important of their presidency, and it's the one thing that they control. But it is risky because if you make a serious mistake, it's like a bad marriage. Only you can't get a divorce."

That was a statement made by former vice president Walter Mondale. After being exhorted to cast his nets into the deep and let down his nets for other potential vice presidents, and after deliberating with his comrades for months with their great seine net but failing to find anyone, the Biden team admitted that it appeared likely that they would find anyone who would meet his requirements.

All humans are helpful or serve a purpose; however, not all humans always serve a purpose. All the women on President Joseph Biden's list were highly qualified. They were all tenderly motherly. All may have gone the additional mile at work, but Joseph R. Biden desired more. He would say I wanted a "simpatico". Like a successful marriage requires agreeable, likable shared qualities, a like-minded, sympathetic man, and a woman, President Joseph needed a "simpatico".

Believing that the woman he formerly competed against was the very candidate who made his heart smile, President Joseph Biden reasoned that not choosing Kamala Harris would be a huge mistake. Her debating skills, qualifications for office, and the racial diversity she would offer to the ticket did not become a point of contention. He just recounted the facts of the matter and then pleasantly added:

"Nevertheless, no other candidate seemed to match the political moment better."

In the end, the only candidate who scored highly with Biden's search committee on so many of their core criteria for choosing a running mate, including her ability to help him win in the 2020 November America election, was Senator Kamala Harris.

I would like every married couple to pretend they are reading aloud a portion of an autobiography they are writing about themselves; each new phase of their lives with its lofty progression.

FOREWORD - 1

Ewuramma, a member of the Church of Pentecost, Bronx District, is a known and an experienced interpreter for the Church of Pentecost, USA.

The first time I met her was when I preached at Bronx Central Church of Pentecost in 2016. She was my interpreter, and honestly, her linguistic prowess caught my rapt attention. I've had many people interpret my preachings but she stood out, with great grace, as the best for interpretation. My admiration of her linguistic potential and grace deepened when I had several one-on-one discussions with her.

Ewuramma majored in Psychology at the Stony Brook University, New York. I am, therefore, not surprised at her literary ability and her questioning expertise. She questions nearly everything constructively and thinks holistically about how to solve challenges. She is a lady with in-depth knowledge of God and the scriptures. My interactions with her gave me a strong conviction that she has garnered various pieces of information and knowledge that would be a literary treasure for generations if put into a book.

She has been an excellent student of the Holy Spirit. I had always wanted to find out how she was able to gather those pieces of in-depth knowledge to come out with this timely book, "As It Was In The Beginning". She simply told me she has held various roles in the Church in which, she thought, the Lord strategically placed her to meet different people with different circumstances so that she could gain the needed experience and knowledge in life.

Ultimately, she describes herself as a student of the Holy Spirit. Many of the things she has exquisitely explored in this book and has given expert advice on attest to the fact that she has been an excellent student of the Holy Spirit. It is remarkably interesting to note that some of the things she has given expert information and guidance about in this book are things she has not personally experienced. It simply has to be the Holy Spirit, the Excellent Teacher who has taken her through to come out with this gem of a book.

"As It Was In The Beginning" is a well thought-out and timely book. The institution of marriage is under serious attack because marriage is no longer looked upon with the lens of God but rather, it is seen in the light of what people believe is right, leading to many challenges. The Office for National Statistics for England and Wales's Divorce statistics for 2019 states that, 60% of marriages end before the 20th wedding anniversary with the average (median) length of marriage at the time of divorce being 12.2 years. The most common reason cited when people petition for divorce is "unreasonable behaviour" which covers a wide range of things, from lack of emotional support, lack of sexual relationship, refusing to contribute financially, domestic abuse and others.

This book, therefore, comes to realign the institution of marriage as ordained by God. It gives a vivid account of the origin and purpose of marriage and suggests how marriage should be re-lived. It also gives various nuggets, snippets and pieces of guidance on singlehood.

The author clearly explains the needed institutions for a successful marriage as the Family, the Church, the Society and the Government or the State. The organised duties and responsibilities of those institutions are meant to solve the challenges that distort the original purpose and establishment of marriage as ordained by God. An effective marriage in essence, depends on a strong Family, the Society, the State and the Church.

The author also places high premium on the roles of both the husband and the wife in a marriage institution. Although equal in value, men and women are not the same role-wise. The role of a man is to be the teacher, judge and administrator and to give specific instructions to specific individuals in the family in addition to making choices while the wife's role is explicitly defined as being that of her husband's companion and helpmeet in carrying out his responsibilities. Marriage is a mystery because it is re-living the relationship between Christ and His Church. The mystery is that like Christ and the Church, the two are in a covenant and each has a part to play to achieve the goals of the covenant.

The author also expounded on marriage as God's institution. The marriage institution, therefore, must always put God first. Every theory on marriage has failed except what the Lord instructed. In this book, the author details God's standards for marriage among others; as between one man and one woman as biologically defined, that a man and woman must be one flesh and that the union of marriage must be permanent and be one spouse and no more.

This book is an extraordinary tool by a gifted individual. It is an excellent resource for provoking thoughts, ideas and actions. I strongly recommend this book because it is timely, well-thought-through, insightful and ideal for training and a reference tool that will guide many in life.

Apostle George Kwaku Korankye,
London South Area, Church of Pentecost UK

FOREWORD - 2

This book is not just another book to increase the stock of books on your shelf, but it has a good spiritual insight that will help the believer to grow in grace and in the knowledge of God.

In chapter one and two, Ewuramma traces the origin of the human race and the usefulness of the scriptures.

She also handles the purpose and plan of the creation of woman; the fact that Eve's delayed creation was not a question of an afterthought but a stratagem; she does that in chapter three.

In the ensuing chapters of the book, she shares the secrets that will help all marriages to succeed.

The reader will find this a gem of a book, which he or she cannot put away, but a mine worth digging to the last depth, to deplete from it its minerals buried underneath. The reader will find in the later chapters a pool of wisdom about the family, the source of human law, how to live for the good of others, the essence of organized society and many more.

Chapter four is where Ewuramma throws light on the responsibility of the family, the place and the sacred role of the parents, and the responsibility of the children to their parents.

One will find chapter five very interesting, where Ewuramma draws parallel a mother's role and that of the church, and God's word about a nation.

In chapter 6, the subject of the two inevitable institutions are handled efficiently; how to handle the tension between the state and the church vis-a-vis the laws of God.

In the subsequent 3 chapters, the book tries to resolve the proper use of the conscience, the mystery of marriage, and the nitty-gritties of the sacred institution. The author concludes with expectations that all marriages, families, homes and churches experience an Eden to the glory of God.

This book is biblical in its underlying doctrine; though some points come from her subjective reflections of the scripture, Ewuramma has kept faithfulness to the fundamental principles of bible doctrine.

The book has a divine touch which the believer will find refreshing. I, thereforere, commend this book highly.

Yaw Adjei-Kwarteng,
Apostle, Church of Pentecost
International Executive Council Member
Area Head, Bompata Kumasi

Endorsements

The Author, in the book, vividly describes how God gave marriage as a gift to Adam and Eve, and hence, humanity in totality. The beauty of creation is such that God, who is perfect, made all things beautiful, and seeing how good it was, handed all His creation to man. Yet, there was the core need of man to have partnership with a *helpmeet*. Here, the writer describes the partnership of a *helpmeet* as the want of the soul. The overarching premise is "It is not good that man should be alone." *Whenever the soul has a desire that God inspires, God intends to fulfill that desire.* Hence, the creation of woman to partner man was not an afterthought of God. God perfectly did it for the continuity of the human race.

The write-up explores the trajectory of divorce and describes it as emanating from Satan and not of God. She, then, explains the need to, therefore, consider the place of solemnity in marriage ceremonies as it helps couples eschew the place of the flesh which turns to dishonor God. The book, further, counsels couples to avoid the wasted hours of promiscuous relationship so that they can embrace the nourishment and the full blessings of God in their respective marriages.

I, therefore, highly endorse this book.

Apostle Mike Kwame Etrue
Area Head, Koforidua
Executive Council Member, Eastern Regional Coordinator
Church of Pentecost

This write-up is full of insightful thoughts about God, creation, marriage, home, family, church and society. The discussion on why and how God spoke other things into existence but formed Adam from the dust is interesting. Much more interesting, perhaps, is why the Lord did not create Eve directly from the dust but from and with some body parts of Adam. The thought that this must have been done so they could be part of and complement each other, inspires discussion on home, family and society. These are developed further in the book.

This is a well-written and a pleasant reading material. Readers will find it enlightening.

Apostle Retired Joseph Kwame Assabil
Former International Executive Council Member Church of Pentecost INT.

Ewuramma has given us practical wealth of wisdom that brings health to relationships and marriage and makes us find fulfillment in life. This book is a masterpiece and a timely divine gift to the world and the body of Christ in a time that our world is woefully plagued with different worldviews and secular humanism ideologies that seek to undermine the sanctity and sacredness of marital institution against God's original intention for mankind. The author's ingenuity to beginning the book by tracing the human race to the creative power of God to reveal His purpose is remarkably espoused to enhance learning.

What sets this book apart among others is the extensive and laborious efforts put into drawing much wisdom and deepening spiritual knowledge and practical lessons about the need of mankind right from creation; the state of singlehood, the rudiments of the institution of marriage according to God's design, the bonding principles of the family unit, human laws emanating from a divine source and the need to live for the good of others as expressed in the quote:

"God's general rule is that by living for other people's welfare, we will also benefit ourselves."

The author's empathetic and compassionate tone and style of writing makes this piece a reflective book, a need assessment and a purposeful companion.

Reading through the book takes your mind through a spiritual adventure of rediscovering the purpose of God for your life and the need of mankind for the fulfillment of life. It also serves as a searchlight that throws light on deep spiritual truths; and then as a guiding light, it brings you illumination to your path for a fulfilling and lasting relationship.

Being in ministry for over 23 years, I find this book useful and a timely piece to bring illumination to both the young and the old, the singles and the married, to help them pay attention to the blueprints of God for their lives, marriages, the family units and a holistic life to enhance proper transitions in life.

Aps. Samuel Edzii Davidson,
Offinso Area Head, The Church of Pentecost.

Endorsements

We are living in the times where absolute truth seems to be fading away. Everyone has their own interpretation to life. Nothing of God has the meaning to its originality. The manual or the compass of life, the Bible, has apparently been ignored. As a result of that, most people find themselves in the state of confusion. The truth is, if there is a creation, then, there must be a Creator. Nothing was created for nothing. Abusing purpose in any kind brings an untold story.

The writer, in her own small way, has suggested some antidote to this social canker by addressing the root causes of the woes of today. Get a copy for your library. This book must be read by all.

Pastor Kwasi Afoakwah-Duah
COP, Galilea District, Ghana

Questions are an important aspect of human life. It is estimated that the average person asks about 20 questions per day. We often refer to different information sources to get answers to some of life's most pressing questions about God, creation, marriage, home, family, church, and society. For instance, "Why did God form man from the dust of the ground but spoke other things into existence?"

It is refreshing that this book, with substance and simplicity, provides a coordinated intersection between those important life concepts. In this write-up, the author draws from the authoritative perspective of the Scriptures on those life issues in conjunction with everyday life lessons to simplify the otherwise complex subject of God, mankind, and our relationships.

This is a well-written and a pleasant reading material. Readers will find it both enlightening and practical. Certainly, it will be of immense benefits to all readers.

Richard Nsiah
New York District Pastor, The Church of Pentecost

I am enthused about the opportunity to read this insightful book, "As It Was in The Beginning", which talks about God, His teachings, His word and His promises.

The writer, through God's infinite wisdom, has given us a well elaborated and educative insight about relationship and marriage and how purposeful it is in the sight of God, and how relevant and essential it is in a healthy society.

Further, the book discusses three purposes of marriage - companionship, procreation and redemption. This masterpiece is a great blessing to the body of Christ and the world at large, especially the young ones who wish to journey on the part of marriage.

It educates both men and women to know their roles and place in marriage as encapsulated in Genesis 2.23: "This is now the bone of my bones and flesh of my flesh she shall be called woman because she was taken out of a man."

Not only does the book talk about marriage, but also, it talks about the origin of the human race, the church of God, the society, family responsibility and many more.

As a mother and a minster's wife, I find this spirit-filled book very useful and refreshing to all souls.

I will, therefore, entreat everyone out there to get a copy.

God bless you.

Mrs. Faustina Anane-Sarfo
Wife of Apostle Isaac Anane- Sarfo,
New York Area Head, Church of Pentecost USA INC.

CHAPTER 01

MARRIAGE IS A GIFT

Marriage is a gift much like eternal life. God is the one who bestows upon us the potential to love and be loved within the institution of marriage. Every human being who has it receives eternal life as a gift. When we initially entered the world, we did not have it. We were born by the first Adam and destined for death. We did not create eternal life or create it from within us through some mysterious process.

It is a gift rather than a domesticated plant planted and nourished on human soil. Therefore, marriage is not given as a reward for good deeds. Since receiving a reward is necessary for doing service, it cannot be a gift.

The word "gift" eliminates any connotation of debt. If something is a gift or a grace, it is no longer an obligation or a recompense. Like eternal life, when God implants it in anyone's soul, it is a free gift of Jesus Christ given to the unworthy rather than the deserving. Therefore, we do not see a justification to divorce or revoke marriage from someone who has already acquired it.

Imagine if a billionaire gave a poor man a $1 million mansion, and shortly after, the man suffered a hip dislocation in an accident. He could continue taking part in the gift like before his hip dislocated. If his latter situation was taken into account in any way, no one would be able to stop him from receiving the benefit any more than they could have stopped him from ever receiving it. The billionaire did not give the poor man the mansion as someone who deserved it; it was a gift. The billionaire had already given the poor man the mansion, so there was no reason to stop him from continuing to live there.

Just like Mephibosheth did not intentionally become handicapped, the poor man did not intentionally injure himself, and as a result, he was permitted to sit at David's table even though he was a lame man.

"David said to him, Fear not, for I will surely show you kindness for Jonathan your father's sake, and will restore to you all the land of Saul your father [grandfather], and you shall eat at my table always" (1Samuel 9:7).

Or why the present tense, as we have it here, should not always be a present fact. Alternatively, if the poor man abused the mansion, the millionaire had given him, the billionaire had the right to rescind the gift if his name was still associated with it and his reputation was tarnished as a result of the poor man's actions.

Without question, marriage is a gift that God never intended to be taken away from anyone. Boredom, communication problems, lack of attention, lack of appreciation, anger issues, unrealistic expectations, division of labor, power inequality, lack of appreciation, stress, and issues are like broken legs and hips in marriages.

Although they may affect the joy of marriage, they are not justifications for a Giver of the gift of marriage to withdraw it from a beneficiary. It is more of a rationale for the husband and wife to adjust to each other based on their experiences and natural tendencies.

The Unknown Giver Of The Gift Of Marriage And The Abused Gifts

There is a story about a president who was already in office and was seeking reelection. It was at a time when the majority of his country, which had supported him in his first election, had grown weary of his administration's lack of effective leadership. Consequently, in accordance with the presidential polls, they planned to flip parties. In a presidential debate with his opponent, the moderator questioned the incumbent president about whether he had made an effort to visit areas where most people planned to change their party affiliation. The country's incumbent president responded:

"Yes, I have, and I believe they are a segment of the country with a short memory, are they not?"

They were the majority that elected him to an office just three years prior, but he claimed he had no idea if that was true or not. The moderator responded:

"Well, I thought they helped you win the previous election and that you had a short memory because you don't seem to remember that there is a saying that says, "Do not bite the hand that feeds you."

Many people's ability to remember those who offer us presents or assist us to improve our lives is negatively impacted by their short-term memory which also has an impact on everything else that is positive. Some people, I worry, have such poor memory that they cannot even remember who gave birth to them. If you are a husband or a wife or in any human relationship, attempt to apply the incumbent president's situation to yourself. Consider whether you can reasonably criticize the president for completely forgetting them despite his having the backing of the majority of the population.

Sadly, the comparison despises a lot of husbands and wives! Many spouses will admit that they are no better off than the incumbent president in the narrative. If it's feasible, their cases contain even more contradictions and inconsistencies.

One is struck by two things while observing some married couples and their interactions with other people, particularly those who lack what the former have. It is difficult to decide which of these two things to be most amazed by. One thing that amazes people is the couple's terrible sin of building idols of themselves. Another thing that amazes people is how they demean those who are either unmarried or do not have happy marriages compared to themselves. Such husbands and wives have all their hearts could desire: God has blessed them with a happy marriage, godly children, successful businesses, and social standing. According to all reports, the lines have fallen into their hands in beautiful settings, and they have a noble legacy.

Instead of being appreciative and remembering that all they have is a gift from God's providence, and instead of asking "Who makes us to differ?", such spouses, instead, become so conceitedly confident.

The world has witnessed the haughtiness of some spouses, their vainness, berating, and boastfulness, and how they have made fun of their unhappy neighbors who either have marital issues or are not married. Wealth and all the other addictions that find a convenient home in the repose of uninterrupted affluence and comfort arose from such pride.

Apostle Paul's question about the varieties among the Corinthians was addressed to the Corinthian church, not the general public.

"For who makes you differ from another? And what do you have that you did not receive? Now if you did indeed receive it, why do you boast as if you had not received it?" (I Corinthians 4:7 NKJV).

They were related to Christians who had been baptized upon professing their faith in Jesus Christ while living in a church-state.

Providence has made many Christians stand out from other Christians. In contrast, many of God's precious and wonderfully beloved children live in abject poverty and lack practically everything. They are not being hunted down, mistreated, or tortured, but they are still starving, and no one is giving them food. They are thirsty, but nobody offers them anything to drink. Their years are lost in hardship, and their lights are wasted in poverty.

There are other God's children who were once wealthy but have now been abruptly reduced to the lowest levels of poverty. They understood what it meant to be valued among the elite, but no man was concerned for them now that they were among the swine.

Many people around the world would behave appropriately if they understood they only had what God gave them. Why should a student at a private college brag about having more debt than a student at a community college who has a smaller loan? Can a private college student who has accumulated $100,000 in a debt claim superiority over a community college student because they have only accumulated $5,000 in debt? Anyone who is wise would disagree. But if they did, they would be as wise as those who boast more than their fellow creatures because they enjoy greater rank, riches, reputation, and status in this world.

"For who makes you differ from another? And what do you have that you did not receive? Now if you did indeed receive it, why do you boast as if you had not received it?" (I Corinthians 4:7 NKJV).

And the more a husband and wife have received from God, the more debt they have. However, going back in time is often the greatest way for many husbands and wives to feel and understand this aspect of the discussion. They will then start to see that a person does not become graced by a course of planning or working. A human being cannot predict the course of grace, and the steps of providence are unknown.

The Hebrew meaning of the name Mary is "Drop of the sea", "Bitterness", and "Beloved". The meaning of Hannah is "Favor" or "Grace." God purposefully favored the Virgin Mary, opened her womb, and converted her into a type of second Eve to give birth to Jesus Christ who is the source of our salvation. The same God also shut Hannah's womb, a legitimate woman who felt the agony of sharing her Husband's love with Peninnah when all the love should have been all for Hannah. Peninnah, who had a quiver full of children, taunted Hannah, the childless mourner. Peninnah, however, was not blessed, whereas Hannah, despite all of her suffering, was treasured by God.

Just an athlete would come from their hiding place and win their race, and the sun which never rises in irregularity to set upon a sudden at its right time, so did Hannah rise to complete God's course.

Hannah and Mary are two women with very different backgrounds, but God worked such amazing miracles through them that their stories have been told throughout history. Godly husbands and wives should begin to express gratitude to God and extend grace to the less fortunate when they reflect on and appreciate the enormous favor that God has shown them.

May spouses be overcome with God's grace and plead the case of those who are seemingly less graced just as the bud opens to the sun of its own volition when it experiences it.

"A human being cannot predict the course of grace, and the steps of providence are unknown."

A Choice To Be An Abigail, A Mrs Job, A Herodias, Or A Jezebel

A person's status of marriage, whether married or unmarried, has nothing, whatsoever, to do with our everlasting destiny: for it is said:

"Most assuredly, I say to you, he who believes in Me has everlasting life." (John 6:47 NKJV).

However, marriage will determine whether so many husbands and wives go to heaven or hell. Consider a scenario in which two passionately religious Alex and Nancy, who have for long been some of the most devout people in Christian history, marry. Let's say that following their marriage, Nancy, instead of submitting to Alex in the Lord, places a higher value on his words at the expense of God - what would the couple be? Do not quote me as saying it to any married couple: Paul is the one who said that anyone who should understand the truth and choose to act in a different way would be – A FOOL.

"O foolish Galatians, who hath bewitched you, that ye should not obey the truth…" (Galatians 3:1)

A man who has a strong will and acts according to their desires are extremely dangerous; a dictator is a dreadful being even if they were so sweet. When the sheep were in the pasture, David and his followers kept an eye on Nabal, a specific shepherder, and his flocks. When it was time to shear the flocks, David sent some of his followers to Nabal's sheepshearing feast to make a plea that money be provided in support of his troops because they had taken care of Nabal's herds, which would have undoubtedly been depleted by systematic plunder.

However, Nabal had already received all the benefits he had hoped for from David and did not hesitate to respond to his messenger in a rude and abrasive way. Nabal said:

"And Nabal answered David's servants and said, Who is David? Who is the son of Jesse? There are many servants nowadays who are each breaking away from his master." (1 Samuel 25:10).

Such a sarcastic remark was inevitable to prick David's emotions; in fact, we are certain that it cut him to the quick. David had not evaded his master, Saul. Although he was separated from Saul, not Saul's enemy, his master had thrown him out, and he was then doing his best to keep the peace. David's blood was boiling. *Let us hear him:*

"Now David had said, Surely in vain have I protected all that this fellow has in the wilderness, so that nothing was missed of all that belonged to him; and he has repaid me evil for good." (1 Samuel 25:21)

David then turned to face his warriors and stated:

"And David said to his men, Every man gird on his sword. And they did so, and David also girded on his sword; and there went up after

David about 400 men, and 200 remained with the baggage." (1 Samuel 25:13).

Then, with David's leading the way, his hot blood on fire inside of him, and his rage visible on his face, 400 men marched out, leaving 200 men to protect the caverns. David said:

"May God do so, and more also, to David if I leave of all who belong to him one male alive by morning." (1 Samuel 25:22).

Without a doubt, David set out with the full intention of defeating Nabal, demolishing the latter's home to the ground, and then wreaking havoc on the sheepherder's estate.

David had a tendency toward impulsivity, and somehow men, with any life in them, occasionally lose their cool. Certain people are as calm, peaceful, and easygoing as a sluggish stream of water. Their moral character is never blown into a rage like the waves of the sea, and their peace most surely does not flow like a river. David was not that kind of a man. He would punish Nabal no matter what. However, as he frantically chases Nabal of Mount Carmel, he encounters a "Woman," Abigail who is Nabal's wife.

I can see David having the hard thought of striking her, but she is a woman, so no. He cannot hit her, and to make matters worse, Abigail is at his feet pleading with him to place the entire guilt on her shoulders.

She, then, continues hoping David won't take offense, by describing her Husband as a very foolish and ungracious man. Abigail brings David a gift, and she tells him that it will bring him great comfort when he becomes king to believe that he has only ever participated in the Lord's battles. She makes David forget the present by constantly bringing up the future. His heart eventually gives way to quiet contemplation, and he begins to behave more like a saint than a soldier sheathing his sword and leaving the situation in the hands of his God.

God, Himself, carried out vengeful justice against the enemy while preventing His servant David from murdering without justification. It wasn't until the practice of physical revenge momentarily subsided that a substantial vengeance became apparent. Ten years later, Nabal died.

For A Marriage To Thrive, It Takes A Man And A Woman

Exaggerating the instrumentality of a woman and her power or usefulness in the family and society does not pose a significant threat. The danger appears to be in the tendency of a man to undervaluing and abusing her or the woman to misusing her power of influence.

Through the power of His unfathomable grace, God has wrought in the hearts of women a burning passion for the salvation of others and a desire to seeing them do the right thing.

Many Christian women have prayed for the conversion of immoral men throughout history to soften their hardened hearts toward compliance and make them aspire to spread the gospel. However, a lot of women have diverted their influence to manipulating their husbands to cause mayhem and create difficulties in their families and communities. A Jezebel would have sought David's murder in Abigail's circumstances. If Mrs. Job were Abigail, she would motivate her Husband to keep fighting his enemies. A Herodias in Abigail's position would have secretly sought an instrument to ask for her Husband's enemy's head. A Sapphira in Abigail's position would have stood by her Husband even though she knew it was wrong.

The fundamental lesson from the lovely union of a husband and a wife is that it can be used positively or negatively depending on the couple's decision. Both the wife and the husband are to be the other's friends. The couple should give each other some healthful counsel and some good and sound advice as friends. As friends, they owe each other much more than just sympathy, as well as a lifetime of selfless devotion to the people whose cause they support.

A husband and a wife should prioritize their friendship as the most loving relationship in the world. Now, only sincere people may form true friendships. The soul of honor is in the heart. A sure evidence of loyalty in a marital friend is when a husband is faithful to his wife and vice versa despite their flaws. Every person should be able to rely on their spouse to point out their shortcomings to them in a caring and polite way. Sinister flatterers and adoring hypocrites are the crumbs and carcasses of friendship in marriage. They are merely the pests that infest the majestic tree of marriage.

When a husband and a wife, however, are close friends in their marriage, they have enough confidence in each other to be open with each other about their shortcomings. Give me a wife or a husband who will be honest with their spouse, who will humbly acknowledge when they are mistaken, and who will not excuse their wrongdoing when it is obvious that it is contrary to God's plan.

True love will correct you when you are in the wrong. Despite the fact that God is loving, He did not ignore Adam and Eve's sin when He knew how terrible it was for them. After the couple had sinned, God came "in the coolness of the day", or, as the Hebrew renders it, "in the wind of the evening". As the evening breeze blew through the garden, the loving God came to Adam and his wife and confronted them. Correcting a loved one who has done something wrong is never easy. You are unsure about their likely reaction.

However, if we are able to follow God's example, then the wife or the husband will always come, in the coolness of the day, while in the chamber of their home. There, they will say to each other, "My dearest, I have observed such-and-such a thing in your behavior that I believe I must advice you of as my spouse." That spouse has proven themselves to be a good friend by acting in that manner. We never receive appreciation when we point out other people's shortcomings; instead, we risk their resentment. Your beloved spouse may occasionally thank you for it if you are courteous, but this does not necessarily make them like you anymore. However, we must keep in mind that every action a spouse takes in a marriage is done to advance the spouse's spiritual growth.

If you truly love your spouse, you will place more importance on where their soul will spend eternity than the house he or she builds on this earth. That mindset will make you more prone to monitor your spouse's relationships with God, others, business transactions, etc. Every Christian may see the choice between heaven and hell as being so simple and straightforward that anyone with even the slightest common sense would know better to choose heaven than to choose hell.

No one, not even a superior being, has to choose between heaven and hell on our behalf. We are free to choose between the two, and God has provided us with relevant understanding and appropriate equipment to make an informed decision. However, we can also support one another in making the best decision.

"A sure evidence of loyalty in a marital friend is when a husband is faithful to his wife and vice versa despite their flaws."

A Resolute Decision

Every Christian husband and wife should always feel joy and elation when they recognize God in all their endeavors. If there is any couple who, thus, ungratefully forget, it should cause them serious reflections, for God does not forget.

"For she has not noticed, understood, or realized that it was I [the Lord God] Who gave her the grain and the new wine and the fresh oil, and Who lavished upon her silver and gold which they used for Baal and made into his image." (Hosea 2:8).

While the child might not remember the mother's generosity, the mother will never forget what she endured while carrying it in the womb and giving birth to the baby. It is possible for a beneficiary to forget what they received, but it is unlikely for the benefactor to forget what they have given. If God's memory keeps track of all He has given a husband and a wife, then let them feel ashamed for letting their memory allow the loss of those things to forget how God restored love to humanity.

When considering what sin has done to humanity, a Christian should have idolatry as their very last consideration. It transformed that lovely Eden, which served as our heavenly garden, into a wasteland and turned us into the children of labor and suffering. What has sin accomplished for mankind? As long as we continue to live in sin, it takes away our beauty, distances us from God, and places blazing cherubim to guard the entrance to the presence of God.

The sin of idolizing marriage will hurt the husband and the wife in their Eden in the short-term or in the long-term. It will ruin them, defile them, and ultimately kill them. Idolatry creates sickness, excavates graves, and produces worms. The idolatry of human sins, which led to Jesus Christ's crucifixion, has the power to kill anyone if it can. May God perform a massive work in the hearts of each husband and wife changing them so that they will uproot the idols they have previously built.

"Idolatry creates sickness, excavates graves, and produces worms."

CHAPTER 02

THE ACTUAL MARRIAGE RACE

We always adhere to the rules and guidelines of the several organizations we are affiliated with in the secular world where we work. The leadership provides us with some rules to follow in order to be affiliated with the organization. We accept them even though we might not agree with some of them. We do this with the understanding that their guidance, however flawed, was, nevertheless, well-intentioned. Even when we cannot receive some of the rules, for the sake of our membership in the organization, the leadership offers it to us, knowing that their training, even should it have been mistaken, was, nevertheless, well meant.

Almost all Christians, whether devout or not, believe that marriage is God-instituted. God has used His marriage to Israel as an analogy for the marriage of Christians. To have happy marriages, we must follow the prescribed route when marrying in a culture of love, peace, forbearance, and adaptability.

In marriage as a "Race", God accompanies the husband and wife to the starting line and passionately urges them to "Let us run" rather than "Run". God, who is love, runs beside every husband and wife. Such a lover's presence is extremely motivating. In a good company, doing good things is a good thing. God says:

"Let us run with patient endurance and steady and active persistence the appointed course of the race that is set before us" (Hebrews 12:1).

From His mouth, God provides the husband-and-wife wings which are set on their heels. Marriage's race has an impact because the husband's and wife's family, friends, tribe, neighbors, community, nation of residence, or nations of origin are all focused on them. The race for marriage is not a week endeavor but a race for the greatest reward.

Angels, powers, and principalities have assembled to witness the wonderful performance that is a husband-and-wife marriage. The Saints who have been redeemed by the blood of Jesus Christ have also gathered. They see couples struggling for holiness and exerting all of their might to imitate Jesus' unselfish love, forgiveness, sacrifice, and acceptance. You will no doubt remember the reason why a bridegroom and a bride say: "May God be our helper" after exchanging their wedding vows.

Marriage must be a difficult race because it also necessitates the disposal of all the baggage from the past.

"Therefore then, since we are surrounded by so great a cloud of witnesses [who have borne testimony to the Truth], let us strip off and throw aside every encumbrance (unnecessary weight) and that sin which so readily (deftly and cleverly) clings to and entangles us..." (Hebrews 12:1).

Every burden of worry and every rag of sin that could divert a husband or a wife from the marriage race must be put aside. Unfortunately, a lot of people enter the marriage race already handicapped. Some husbands have broken legs when they are married, and some wives have broken hands. So how can two feeble individuals compete in a race like marriage? Even the beginning is beyond the husband's and wife's ability; imagine how much more endurance must go beyond their capacity! Oh, how a bridegroom and bride are expected to depend on the power of the Holy Spirit and to accept free grace!

The race that is put in front of them makes the husband's and wife's helplessness and hopelessness, in the absence of divine grace, most apparent. The race of marriage very much demands stamina from the husband and wife while also promoting unity, sanctity, love, and submission, exposing their frailty. The couple is obliged to kneel and pray to God the Strong One for strength before they have even started running. In this race, I humbly implore every husband and wife to concentrate only on God's Actual Terms for the Marriage Race.

"The race of marriage very much demands stamina from the husband and wife while also promoting unity, sanctity, love, and submission, exposing their frailty."

GOD'S ACTUAL TERMS OF THE RACE OF MARRIAGE

Whether we are knowledgeable about all of their names or not, there are actual Terms of the actual marriage. God actually created the Actual Terms governing the Actual institution of marriage. When you hear many married couples' positive and negative testimonies, marriage first appears to be a, somewhat, frightening institution.

It is easier - and unquestionably more effective - to familiarize ourselves with the Actual God and the Actual Terms of the Actual Marriage Race than trying to understand every detail of marriage. In His own Terms (Language), God, who established marriage from the beginning, said in two separate places which are here joined:

"He created them male and female and blessed them and named them [both] Adam [Man] at the time they were created. Therefore a man shall leave his father and his mother and shall become united and cleave to his wife, and they shall become one flesh" (Genesis 5:2; Genesis 2:24).

Terms of the Race: Every man and every woman who registers to compete in the marriage race must be concerned only with what the Founder of marriage says about becoming one flesh. There is no a dictionary one can consult to clarify the meaning of each phrase used or each unused word or behavior in a marriage. Hence, everyone in the marriage race should bear in mind that there is only one Actual Term, and all other language is just conversation.

And every husband and wife can appreciate their calling into the marriage race far better when they compete on the Actual Terms of the Actual Marriage Race than by comparing themselves to people who consider themselves to be "specialists" in marriage. A prospective spouse may be indifferent or uninterested in certain "experiences" of marriage or specific people who identify as "specialists" in marriage when they live their lives perfectly in God's presence and work to become familiar with the Actual Terms of Marriage.

The Bible makes God's terms clear and makes His Holy Spirit accessible to anyone who seeks Him. God has also made many godly married couples available, and they have and are continuing to flourish by adhering to the Real Terms of the Real Marriage institution. Therefore, neither a husband nor a wife should dare to back out of the actual marriage contest.

But how are they supposed to start a race for which they are so unfit? Who is going to lend a hand? Who should they turn to in difficult situations? Does not every one of these questions brilliantly lead every married couple and Christian to the verse in the Bible where it reads:

"Looking away [from all that will distract] to Jesus, Who is the Leader and the Source of our faith [giving the first incentive for our belief] and is also its Finisher [bringing it to maturity and perfection]. He, for the joy [of obtaining the prize] that was set before Him, endured the cross, despising and ignoring the shame, and is now seated at the right hand of the throne of God". (Hebrews 12:2)

Keep To God's Terms

Our world is a world of terms. I would invite any person to point to any sentence in the Bible where there is no strong, emphatic repetition and accumulation of terms that convey the most perfect and absolute terms between God and humanity. Throughout a Christian's days of life, God proposes to us in terms of love, grace, and peace. And the only terms upon which God can deal with guilty men are terms of mercy:

"...O God, be favorable (be gracious, be merciful) to me, the especially wicked sinner that I am!" (Luke 18:13).

When we are praying, we stand on praying ground and plead on the terms with God. As best as they could, a preacher pleads with the sinner in God's name on the terms of salvation and damnation of the soul who refuses to repent. Because God meets us on many terms, we have become accustomed to dealing and speaking in terms with our fellow beings.

We say someone is or is not a person of love if they do not speak in such terms as a loving person speaks. We are familiar with terms; therefore, we have the terms of a contract, the terms of tenancy, the terms of a church or a club membership, an Act of Congress, a concept, a covenant, the terms of business activity, or any other membership (in traditional "terms"), etc. are all examples of "terms". Covenants, contracts, and other concepts are expressed in words in a nominal, traditional manner. Therefore, the words have Grammatical, habitual, and moral (customary) meanings (connotations).

Due to the fact that they frequently "mean very different things in very different contexts", they are all essentially chosen and often quite undefined. Because of that, authorities must be set up to "decide" and "explain" what they mean after they have really been used: why not before? All of those concepts "are simply Grammatical terms; they are names connected to other "pieces of speech".

The Merriam-Collegiate Webster's Dictionary provides definitions for more than 225 words. Additionally, many more dictionaries provide lists of Grammatical Terms, words, names, and other forms of speech. Many people very honestly apply words and terms and connect them to whom they speak or write in the plainest terms. Such a husband or a wife, when they call each other "Honey", they mean it. Such a friend, when they call you "Beloved Friend", they mean every word that drops from their lips.

Such people do not use words they do not mean, and neither do they use words that are not true. However, experience has proven that there are people in our world and the institution of marriage who always unwisely call everybody "Honey this" and "Honey that" when they do not mean an iota of the words that fall from their lips. Come to think of it; sometimes, people do not respond to us on Jesus' terms because of the specific graces and personal qualities that Christians possess.

Not every Christian act of love, respect, or trust on Jesus' terms has benefited a godly husband or wife because there are imposters who try to pass for the real thing.

By natural progression, both unbelievers have spoken on Jesus' terms and lured many godly people into marriage. They used the Christian jargon, "Hallelujah", "Praise the Lord", and "God loves you" because they think that, possibly, by such talk, they could get something out of Christians. They use those unctuous terms without meaning them in their heart. Have we not known husbands and wives call each other *sweetheart* and *honey* when all the while they were emotionally and physically killing each other slowly?

CHAPTER 03

EVERYONE DESERVES LOVE

Once upon a time, it was quite attractive to see every cheek; all bespattered with tears in a marriage. Yet, that wife's eyes, which the husband used to find lovely and enjoyed, are now worn out from waiting and watching and are crimson from crying. There is an adage that says: "No one marries their enemy." Everyone, but especially women, inherently desire love. We cry out for love as soon as we come into the world, and we often die still crying out for love. Every human's heart and mind crave for love in one way or another.

Most people just communicate their desire for love in a way that gives the impression that the desire for love is inappropriate. We are created with the feeling that we are loved. God's love has greatly spoiled every immortal soul in humans for the world.

"For God so greatly loved and dearly prized the world that He [even] gave up His only begotten (unique) Son, so that whoever believes in (trusts in, clings to, relies on) Him shall not perish (come to destruction, be lost) but have eternal (everlasting) life" (John 3:16).

Correspondingly, when someone lives a truly Christian life, they also recognize the love of Christians as being unique. Because a Christian has a specific love for all Christians even though they are all motivated by a sense of universal goodwill and desire to love and help everyone.

For the sake of Jesus Christ, the true Christian is said to have a love for the persecuted, maligned, and despised people of God. We are encouraged to love them all, even when we believe some of them are inadvertently making minor mistakes. A true Christian must show love to both mature and infant Christians and even to Christians whose shortcomings are more obvious than their virtues. True Christians hold that they should love every other Christian not because of their status or inherent friendliness, but because Jesus loves them, and they love Jesus. Christians who have, thus far, succeeded in their pursuit of loving and being loved as Christians are gratified.

I want us to consider the disappointment of a Christian man or a woman who believes - or is led to believe - that they have met another Christian who shares their faith, love, joy, patience, forbearance, etc. As a result, they make a commitment to live their entire lives with them, only to discover after the honeymoon stage of the marriage or years after the marriage that the virtue they perceived was either deception or never existed.

Seasons Of Marriage

The little world of marriage is a microcosm of the seasons of the year. No matter what time of year it is in the actual world, every marriage starts in the summer in the marriage world. While the bridegroom and bride look to themselves through the God-given sunshine that promises them happiness, the most pleasant summers always smile upon them. It is a stage in a marriage when the spouses describe their beloved's characteristics in great detail;

when neither spouse is tied to simply saying: "He or she is entirely wonderful."

At this point in their marriage, the spouses take pleasure in discussing the charms of each other's features and daydream about the beauty of their features and personalities. The couples may brag about each other for as long as they like and give each other as much praise as they can during the honeymoon phase of a marriage, but you will never find out that they have exaggerated their own virtues.

You will be astounded by their excellence as they go into great depth about themselves and dwell with great minuteness on everything regarding their allure, strength, character, remarks, and actions.

A loving spouse will generally take care of the other during the summer season of marriage; this is never imposed upon them but it is always enjoyable. During the summer season of marriage, the husband and the wife come up with a thousand ideas of things they can do for each other's comfort, some of which are completely superfluous and would never be required by any kind of legislation. However, their tender hearts urge them to carry them out in order to make each other happy.

But no matter what, summer, with its blossoming flowers, fruit-forming buds, and maturing fruit, never lasts forever. Even though a husband and wife's life may bear many fruits during the summer, this won't stop fall from coming; on the contrary, it will encourage it. The marriage then enters the winter season after the couple has enjoyed the fall season together. During the winter seasons in a marriage, the wind of the law rushes forth against one or both of the spouses when every hope is tumbled, when all the joyous seeds lie deep beneath the dreary soils of despair, and when their souls are tightly bound like a river bound by ice, without tides of joy or of celebrations of love.

God is so gracious that eventually, He causes the gentle wind to blow into the marriage upon the spouse's soul, the waters of desire are instantly released, the spring season of love begins, the flowers of hope appear in their hearts, the trees of faith sprout new shoots, the season of the singing of birds arrives in their hearts, and they experience joy and peace in their belief in Jesus Christ. God graciously arranges it so that the marriage's joyful springtime is followed by a prosperous summer when the husband and wife's graces are in blossoms like fragrant flowers, filling the air with fragrance, and fruits of the Spirit like mangoes and grapes swell into their full proportion in the amiable sunlight of Righteousness.

Then comes in the marriage the spouse's fall season when their fruits grow ripe, and their fields are ready for harvest; the time has come when their God shall gather His "pleasant fruits" together and store them in heaven. There is a time in the marriage when death sets a divorce between a loving couple. And God has given us memory so that we might reflect on the past and use our memories for introspection, recollection, and repentance.

When a spouse encounters marital challenges like a gloomy winter of child disobedience, spousal illness, job loss, and financial difficulties, and they battle in prayer - when the fair spring of hope gradually descends upon them, and their joys start to abound, they will be able to consider God's mercies and love for them and will be able to praise Him for it.

Winter may be just around the corner for some couples, but they are unaware of it. They must be thankful that they do not, as doing so might have worsened their misery. Additionally, the prospect of future pain may make their today's pleasure appear less delightful.

There is a season for everything, and everything has a purpose in existence. Nature's purpose is instruction, not just to entertain and please us. God's four evangelists are spring, summer, fall, and winter. They each deliver a unique interpretation of the same life lesson. HUMAN nature can handle enough for today.

"…Sufficient for each day is its own trouble". (Matthew 6:34).

No husband or wife would have wanted to get married if they had been required to travel to a specific location before getting married so they could raise a veil and foresee every minute detail of the marriage.

Because many spouses could not imagine that a simple joke may enrage a spouse, another spouse will observe and find it difficult to accept that their spouse will forget their anniversary. One spouse couldn't understand why the other would be upset all day. The other spouse could not imagine the lateness of one spouse in picking up a child from school. Another spouse might not believe that their in-law will disrespect them. One spouse will see their spouse being injured in an accident. Another spouse will see their partner's demise and her husband leave their spouse alone. The list is endless. All of those, although strengthening marriage, shouldn't ever be a reason for a marriage to dissolve, but one of them has been blamed for thousands, if not millions, of marriages' terminating.

God's choice to conceal the realities of marriage's shortcomings should make spouses satisfied. They should, thus, rejoice that because it is concealed, its inevitable future suffering has no effect on their day-to-day happiness. The knowledge of a spouse's marriage intricacies and the seasons is not a good thing. It is best for them to understand that the Father is in control of their lives, their marriage, and the seasons that surround them:

"...It is not for you to become acquainted with and know what time brings [the things and events of time and their definite periods] or fixed years and seasons (their critical niche in time), which the Father has appointed (fixed and reserved) by His own choice and authority and personal power" (Acts 1:7).

"...summer, with its blossoming flowers, fruit-forming buds, and maturing fruit, never lasts forever."

THE "PHYSICIANS AND THE SICK" (HUSBAND AND WIFE) OF A MARRIAGE

Every husband or every wife is both a patient and a physician, and their marriage is a hospital. A physician needs to be stationed where there are patients for them to cure. Therefore, when two infallible people are married, there need to be all types of curing and mending. Even when someone becomes a Christian, there is still sin in us.

"Now if I do what I do not desire to do, it is no longer I doing it [it is not myself that acts], but the sin [principle] which dwells within me [fixed and operating in my soul]." (Romans 7:20).

Sin and death as a result of sin entered human beings when Satan entered the Garden of Eden with his temptation. Part of Jesus Christ's mission was to heal us of our sin-related illnesses. But the sin that He heals us of is not simply a matter of routine or practice but rather something inside us. It is much worse than that since sin is present throughout the entire human being, including the heart and nature. When you insert a clean swab into mortal human nature, it will always come out contaminated. We were immersed in sin while still in our mother's womb, and it has since permeated every part of us.

Sin is ingrained in human nature like embedded colors; the more you wash the cloth, the more vividly you see them, but you can never wash them out. Because sin is not an essential component of the human nature as God intended, it is a disease. It is abnormal and was not a part of human nature at first.

Sin is similar to illness in that it throws all human faculties out of whack and upsets the balance of life energies just as illness affects every aspect of our physical being. Sin is infectious, and we have contracted many more sins from our fellow humans that we previously did not have. Through our interactions with other sinners, we pick up many sins that we may not have committed otherwise.

So now you know why a husband and wife are both patients and physicians. Despite the fact that they are both contagious since they are also physicians, they may treat each other. No human being is fully informed of the complexity of the human heart or soul. The physicians at our hospitals must be skilled at tracing sickness to its hidden source and guiding it through all of its cryptic routes in the complex human body. However, the challenge facing the husband and wife who must deal with souls and hearts is even more difficult.

"The heart is deceitful above all things, and it is exceedingly perverse and corrupt and severely, mortally sick!" (Jeremiah 17:9).

Because sin is more subtle than the virus that causes the fatal disease, and because of the way it interacts with every human power, it is even more amazing than the weird effects of viruses like COVID-19 and pest on the human body.

As physicians, the husband and wife must be, somewhat, familiar with each other's diseases knowing the disease is a prerequisite for understanding the cure. So, once a husband and wife start living together, they are aware of each other's disease and its symptoms. When a husband diagnoses his wife's symptoms of insecurities, he must prescribe security medication for her. When the wife diagnoses her husband's anger, she also gives him a prescription for patience. Neither a husband nor a wife can observe the illnesses of the other from a distance. They share a single roof and walk among themselves as they sit, stroll, sleep, and eat.

The husband or wife who simply rushes through the hospital of marriage is very similar to an unqualified doctor who might swiftly go through a hospital without carefully caring for the patients who are lying on beds. However, a husband and a wife who decide to live out the rest of their lives side by side in the very center of each other's disease will see it in all of its manifestations. They will see all of their symptoms in forms that no other human has seen or will see. The husband and wife might see each other's diseases as satanic shapes because sometimes, if not most times, when one of them is upset, it might seem all hell has broken loose for a split second. However, the spouse who assumes the role of a physician in that circumstance will speak softly to the sick spouse.

"A soft answer turns away wrath, but grievous words stir up anger". *(Proverbs 15:1).*

In certain cases, the husband and wife will see each other's disease at its worst. However, the couple should cure each other's illnesses with all spiritual and physical instruments.

The husband or wife in the hospital is not an objective observer. They need to continue to study the entirety of every case that comes to the Triage of the Marriage hospital. Even though the human heart is deceiving, the husband and wife will be informed by relying on the power and help of the Holy Spirit. With the help of the Holy Spirit, they will know and understand everything, no matter how unpredictable it is in its many manifestations or how extraordinarily diverse it is in its consistently changing shapes. Their lifelong marriage, or anticipated lifelong marriage, in the marriage hospital, has to teach them about each other's diseases due to their combined nature. Therefore, they will be aware of which diseases necessitate surgical intervention and can be treated without inpatient hospitalization.

Both the husband and the wife should be familiar with each other. They ought to be more familiar with each other than even the most experienced surgeon can be through experimentation because theirs is based on experience rather than theory. They have experienced each other's diseases and sorrows together. As a result, the husband and the wife are now each other's patient, physician, and medicine. Their natural selves have blended together and each other's emotions enable the other to do their work perfectly.

Every pain they experience teaches them something, and every pulse of agony makes them wiser to each other. And every sign of irritation of each makes the other more effective in carrying out the purposes of God in uniting them as a husband and a helpmeet. The husband and the wife, whose job and occupation it is to care for sick souls, make it their main goal to serve as God's instruments in bringing sick souls to believe in the treatment from the great Father, God who has made all healing possible in the person of the great Physician Jesus Christ.

CHAPTER 04

"CONVERSION" OF THE MAN'S LOVE AND THE WOMAN'S SUBMISSION

Because God intended marriage to be irrevocable, marriage, separation, and divorce are incredibly difficult subjects for both Christians and non-Christians. I want to use two well-known analogies to Christians: backsliding and apostasy, to catch your attention and hopefully provoke reflection, even if it is not initially understood.

A man's love was turned away from a woman, and her submission was turned away from him. Since the tragic day that our first parents disobeyed God's commandment, both sexes have been complicit in the same criminal offense. All of the men and women stood as a symbol of humanity turning our back on one another and traveling down a destructive path. All that was necessary for a man to fall in love with a woman and for a woman to submit to him was a 180-degree turn in each other's direction.

The love of the man and the submission of the woman needed to hear the order "Right about turn", and to march in the opposite direction from any other direction they had ever marched.

The definition of the word "converted" in this context is "right about turned" which refers to a man's love for a woman and a woman's submission to a man. The Scriptures of attraction cause a man's love and a woman's submission to be converted causing a man and a woman to see that God made them for each other. There are billions of billions of men and women in the world who are heading in the wrong direction, but those two are drawn to each other and seem to be turning in the right direction.

As long as a man or a woman is not ready to marry, they become blind. They cannot see the one that is meant for them. But when the Holy Spirit comes to them and reveals the law of attraction, then the man can perceive that he has a missing rib, and the woman perceives she has a whole to fill on the man's body. Then the Word of God continues to take the man off from all attempts to getting around in the wrong ways. When a man knows that he is going wrong, his instinct leads him to seek to get right by getting to know more about the woman; so, he is attracted.

The Word of God shows the man how he might get right by taking the right steps toward courting the woman. But the Word of God does more than that. If the woman he is courting is a divinely appointed woman for him, in the power of the Holy Spirit, the Word helps the man to believe she is the right woman. Maybe at first, he will be quite staggered at the idea of spending the rest of his life with her - instantaneous love - the giving away of his whole heart to one woman among the billions of women in the world all for nothing - such a commitment to a stranger. The man says, "Surely, it is too risky a thing to commit to." He is filled with a dilemma, for the love and commitment to marriage are deep and mysterious. The Word then comes to him and says:

"Come now, and let us reason together, says the Lord. Though your sins are like scarlet, they shall be as white as snow; though they are red like crimson, they shall be like wool" (Isaiah 1:18).

As the man goes through this process, the woman goes through hers, befitting for submission to the man. And when the Word has completed the process of converting the man and woman, his love and her submission become converted. For when a man looks to his woman alone and the woman looks to her man alone, there is a conversion. That represents conversion and regeneration.

Therefore, in a marriage, the woman and the husband make the appropriate turns in each other's direction. God's marriage with the Jews is presented to us as a brilliant example. It guides us in understanding how relationships inevitably experience ups and downs. There is not a perfect marriage in the world because it was impossible for the infallible, perfect God to maintain a perfect marriage with the fallible Jews.

Given our confidence that God foreknows everything, we cannot help but conclude that He was mindful of the Jews' lack of loyalty before marrying them. Therefore, it is safe to say that despite being extremely painful, the Jews' unfaithfulness was a major means by which God would demonstrate His infinite love and glorify Himself. Knowing in advance that the Jews would be unfaithful, God was keen to make the arrangement by which He would woo His chosen wife out of their ruins, a demonstration of all of His nature and attributes, including love, forbearance, patience, loyalty, etc.

When we observe in the Jews the gracious dealings of a covenant-keeping God, God's handling of them serves as a model for us. His approach to loving the Jews contains a faint hint of naivety.

> *"There is not a perfect marriage in the world because it was impossible for the infallible, perfect God to maintain a perfect marriage with the fallible Jews."*

Every Marriage Has Its Unique Problems

Every thoughtful person can agree that if God had allowed one woman to be married to an identical twin man, the marriage would have been considerably different. No two marriages are identical. Any other being cannot foresee the future status of marriage but God because it is not immediately apparent.

Marriage, one of the most important life events, has a distinction with different methods of dealing with people. Because of this, only God - not a marriage counselor - can establish a marriage without problems. It also goes without saying that it is, somewhat, unnatural for anyone to judge and compare other people's marriages with married couples who are having problems without hearing all sides of their story.

The state of things in our world, including the weather, pandemics, sickness, death, and business, provides a clear and illuminating parable that would be unwise to disregard. God has not allowed any human being to be able to predict the future, know the times and seasons, or draw a map of it. God has often predicted the future by communicating through His prophets. I do not need to give you even one example of the countless times that the Spirit of God used the prophets to prophesy events that were impossible to predict and exceedingly implausible but still happened as they were predicted.

But in the case of marriage, God does not call people to enter expecting to be a prophet or a foreteller of what will happen tomorrow in terms of the marriage, their spouses, their children, their in-laws, or the nations of the world. God has not given us any ability to predict the future. He reveals the past to us so that we may make reparations, but he keeps the future a secret so we can speculate.

BACKSLIDERS IN THE MARRIAGE INSTITUTION

My goal in this particular part is to be the Holy Spirit's tool for awakening, edifying, and rehabilitating backsliders in the marriage institution. Marriage backsliding is a very prevalent problem, much more so than we might think. Many Christians in positions of authority in churches may be guilty of it themselves while still leading hearts to believe that they prosper in a godly marriage.

The way that Satan makes apostasy in the marriage institution to be highly appealing to human nature is similar to how the cunning hunter always makes the entrance into his holes most easy and enticing but always renders it most difficult for his victim to escape.

Almost all marriage separations and divorces began with trivial or little things (Genesis 19:20). According to research, treating your spouse like a child, taking the other person for granted, not listening, and not taking complaints seriously are the top five factors that destroy marriages quickly.

Despite their seeming insignificance, they are powerful weapons Satan uses to pull down the walls in marriage. Now, if a husband would only realize how detrimental treating his wife like a child is; or if a wife had known what would happen if she took her husband for granted, they could have decided to put up with excruciating pain rather than ruin her marriage. Everything about which Satan asks: *"Is it, not a small one?"* must surely contain something horrifying in the end.

When the eyes of a husband and a wife are opened by divine grace, they can see a whole purgatory sleeping soundly in even the smallest negligence in marriage. Because of their microscopic eyesight which allows them to see a world of sin concealed in a single act, idea, or imagination of evil, they avoid it with fear, pass by it, and refuse to interact with it.

The husband and the wife that disregarded the writing on the wall regressed. But unfortunately, without grace, no human foot could ever make full progress on the path of return from backsliding in a marriage institution since it is exceedingly difficult to tread.

I pray that I will effectively draw attention to the decline in the human and divine aspects of marriage life in this section of the book, particularly in bringing the issue to the attention of those it most concerns, namely those who are backsliding in their marriages due to idolatry, negligence, abuse, etc.

There are many such wandering spouses and wives. Their honeymoon romance is gone, and their fervor for the marriage has been snuffed out. Some spouses might have gone even further and completely abandoned their spouses and children. Despite the fact that their spouse still loves them, they no longer care about or are committed to their marriage. And even when their spouse shows them love and forgiveness just as regularly, the mystical ties of gratitude do not bind them to their spouse.

Instead, they have abandoned their loving and caring spouses in favor of the basic love of the most repulsive. However, their spouses have not yet filed for divorce or separated from the beloved they have shared their entire lives with.

I pray that the voice of Israel's God, who suffered abuse and an unfaithful spouse firsthand, may speak to a wandering spouse on behalf of every abandoned spouse.

"That is to say, If a man puts away his wife and she goes from him and becomes another man's, will he return to her again? [Of course not!] Would not that land [where such a thing happened] be greatly polluted? But you have played the harlot [against Me] with many lovers—yet would you now return to Me? says the Lord [or do you even think to return to Me?" (Jeremiah 3:1).

"...treating your spouse like a child, taking the other person for granted, not listening, and not taking complaints seriously are the top five factors that destroy marriages quickly."

APOSTASY IN MARRIAGE

Every single sin, even spouse abuse, demonstrates that Satan has dominion over the individual's soul. All unconverted people are actually under the influence of the devil in some way because he has taken up residence in their hearts where he rules and controls the organs of their bodies.

Many people who have witnessed Satanic possession can undoubtedly attest that some spouses display symptoms that are strikingly similar.

It is very common for Satan to possess one or both spouses and harass them severely and their families. Jesus Christ has defeated Satan and won a victory over him. And every Christian also shares in His victory. His victory covers every Christian like a canopy does for those who are underneath it.

Satan cannot, therefore, possess a Christian, but he may oppress them through harassment. His control over physical bodies has been severely curtailed; instead, he employs the same thing in a harsher form, notably sin's control over people's minds. And in the overwhelming majority of instances where a spouse resists all counsel to stop abusing their spouse, Satan may have returned to seize total control of their heart for a number of reasons, most notably backsliding from the institution of marriage.

The primary objective of Satan is to turn every child of God away from God. In this circumstance, he converts a spouse's heart into an apostate's heart, as a result of which they violently plunge towards doom like a swine possessed by the devil:

"...the [demon] spirit that still constantly works in the sons of disobedience [the careless, the rebellious, and the unbelieving, who go against the purposes of God]" (Ephesians 2:2)

Judas kissed Jesus Christ whiles betraying Him. Most apostates behave in this manner always with a kiss. Every apostate poem, movie, or novel starts with deep regard for love and the truth. And with a kiss, the apostates within betray the beloved.

Most abusive relationships and marriages start out with a nauseating amount of humility, with such sweetness and softness in the cream, sugar, golden syrup, and other delicacies that the committed person might never detect any malice. Cite me as saying:

"Despite how modestly and gracefully they intrude into the lives of kind-hearted, innocent people, many spouses conceal terrible venom."

Satan exploits those types of spouses as a tool for harassing Christians. They become the devil's assistants in the marriage and serve as trustworthy and practical weapons. Tragically, there are many recipients of the gift of marriage that God must take away from them to prevent the gift from harming them and others.

It is dreadful when a gift is used as a weapon for murder; it's very thought to cause a person to become numb and numbingly cold. Many husbands and wives report that they have felt like they have been living under rocks their entire marriages. However, they continue to put up with the marriage that has both cooled them and cast an unbearably moist chill around them, as if death's grip has been on them and it is cold inside them, out of fear of what people will say about them if they file for divorce.

On the other side, many spouses who have quickly escaped such a frightening situation because it tends to make them feel ill and ultimately result in their deaths have been isolated, stigmatized, and criticized. Many abused and seemingly imprisoned husbands and wives, even when they have the ability to escape, choose not to do so out of fear of losing their church positions. Many also fear being isolated from friends and families. In those situations, they are left with little choice but to follow the shadow cast by the death's wing.

No one knows the conditions that many godly husbands and wives are subjected to in their homes.

"My life is among lions; I must lie among those who are aflame—the sons of men whose teeth are spears and arrows, their tongues sharp swords" (Psalm 57:4).

Many husbands and wives who used to be devoted Christians have suddenly turned into lions that regard their spouses as prey which is an enemy. An enemy that is much stronger than its prey — possibly strong in the jaw — and is extremely strong when it comes to biting, ripping, and tearing. The victimized spouse in such a situation is forced to live with spouses who openly flaunt their adultery and blasphemies against them. Alas, it is terrible for them to have their young children among such lions.

The once-loving spouse who has morphed into a lion is strong and cruel, and this real cruelty exposes well-intentioned wives and husbands to criticize and slander. Such spouses are so wicked that if the law permitted it, they would kill one another.

Similar to how the lion sneaks up on its prey before making a quick jump, many spouses sneak up on their vulnerable spouses before springing upon them if they can capture them at an unguarded moment. If the Lionized spouse senses they have found a flaw in their victimized spouse, they attack them with all of their strength.

Unfortunately, many husbands keep an eye on their wives and are prepared to attack them if they can overhear them talking or rile them up and get them to say something stupid. Many wives also exaggerate their husbands' shortcomings, put them under a microscope with a million times more power, and make a big deal out of it. *They exclaim: "I caught him", I have got him."*

They routinely complain to their neighbors about everything that will make their husband or wife look bad since it makes them feel good. Any spouse's freedom, comfort, and happiness in such a situation will be like an eclipsed sun. And they will crouch down in the cold, gloomy, moist darkness of a dreadful sadness and tremble at the chilling touch of uncertainty. Many SPOUSES have an attack of love fever, are frightened, and have started acting irrationally.

All those spouses who are constantly being scrutinized, teased, mistreated by their spouses, and hampered in all that is good and gracious go before the God they serve and cry to Him: *"My soul is among lions."*

God is always more intelligent and powerful than Satan, and His compassion consistently outsmarts Satan.

"Most abusive relationships and marriages start out with a nauseating amount of humility, with such sweetness and softness in the cream, sugar, golden syrup, and other delicacies that the committed person might never detect any malice."

THE BATTERED SPOUSE AND THEIR CHILDREN

Many married couples regard marriage as a den or a prison house where there just awaits an alarm to which they can "Escape for their lives." Despite their best efforts, they loathe the spouse they share a home with since their spouses have turned into a ruthless tyrant that mercilessly devours them. Such victims of relationships are often women and children who are amiable in their temper and excellent in their deportment. However, they are treated as slaves and harlots. And unless Jesus Christ has pity upon them, they die untimely deaths.

Many hearts become sick nigh unto death with the terrible stories of abusive marriages many people, especially Christians, endure. Many married couples cannot ever identify with an abused spouse. And they ought to be very thankful to God that they are spared from those horrific experiences. Blessed are the spouses who have godly spouses and who dwell in Christian families.

They and their children ought to grow like the flowers in a conservatory where killing frosts and biting blasts are unknown. They live under very favorable circumstances. Their soul is among angels; for they dwell where God is worshipped, where family prayer is not forgotten. They dwell where they can have kind guidance in the hour of difficulty and comfort in the time of trial. What a happy circumstance it is when a godly, gracious man has an equally godly and gracious wife.

Alas, not every spouse or child can say the same. Their homes are very much like a zoo because of the lion they live with. And they cry:

"My life is among lions; I must lie among those who are aflame—the sons of men whose teeth are spears and arrows, their tongues sharp swords." (Psalm 57:4)

Many Christians are married to unbelievers. And because of their bad marriages, even the best of spouses have been maligned.

When a husband and a wife have a fundamentally different perspective on God - when one reveres Him, and the other does not - their relationship may become unhealthy. What a burden it is for a Christian to be married to an uncompromising non-believer?

Some spouses have physically assaulted their spouses much as lions attack their prey. Some spouses behave like teachers. They see their married house as a place where they only need to provide knowledge. They are the only family members who are not in the school. Such a self-styled schoolmaster considers the people of their family wholly under their control as students. They, therefore, see no other choice but to spank them for even the smallest infraction of an instruction. These spouses are typically quite rigorous and stern; they often and mercilessly wield the lash, and the conditions of their family members are occasionally no better than slavery.

Every household member is constantly afraid (as was intended to be for their benefit). Even their activities are restricted, and the gloomy schoolteacher's spouse keeps an eye on them. They are strictly always restrained becoming disciplined for the struggle of life. Those spouses have harsh facial expressions and suppress any evidence of comfort or delight in their spouse and children. They equip themselves with punishments but lack compassion and love. The spirits of many spouses and children are broken, and their liveliness is constrained because of such spouses.

THE CRY OF THE BATTERED SPOUSE AND CHILDREN

The soul of the man is the true person; even though some people just focus on the physical body, any injury done to the body ultimately impacts the soul. Sometimes, tears can be vile things that come from a cowardly spirit. Some people cry when they ought to be nostrils flaring their brows. In many instances, married couples cry when they ought to submit to God's will and improve their marriages.

However, an abused spouse's and children's tears often serve as a measure of their helplessness. Their internal sorrow causes their hearts to ache, and the horror of their abusive marriage descends upon me.

A virtuous spouse, who sees their marriage on the edge of disintegrating, experiences fear and trembling. The terror of it overcomes them. Women tend to take marriage issues quite personally for some reason. A godly woman is greatly distressed to watch their marriage crumble. Many worldly people take that unfortunate event in stride with pleasant composure. But it is viewed as a horrible misfortune by the godly.

And those who experience it endure the most agonizing emotions. Alas! Owing to the nature of humans, some people who were blessed with happy marriages are often guilty of callous haughtiness and mocking taunts directed towards couples whose marriages Satan is targeting.

So, godly women with marital issues, sometimes, cannot speak about it. They cannot tell even their fellow Christians about their trouble:

"The poor and needy are seeking water when there is none; their tongues are parched with thirst. I the Lord will answer them; I, the God of Israel, will not forsake them." (Isaiah 41:17).

They are ashamed to tell others what they endure in their marriage and home. It is a sad state for any woman to be in, yet many are in it. And Satan has convinced many women who have done nothing wrong but are victims of abuse to feel guilty. He has made them believe it is their fault that their spouses abuse them.

Therefore, they cannot tell their fellow Christians anything about their condition; so, they miss one useful means of comfort. But even though they are unable to articulate their emotions to people, they can pray to God without using words, and He will still hear them.

"And it shall be that before they call I will answer; and while they are yet speaking I will hear" (Isaiah 65:24).

What? They are unable to talk; so, how is it even possible?

"… their tongues are parched with thirst. I the Lord will answer them" (Isaiah 41:17).

In the very silence of the soul of the battered spouse and child, they speak with God. There is a certain type of communication that blends wonderfully with silence: the speech of grief which displays the misery's wounds, the brokenness of the heart with sobbing. It is the setting before God of the intolerable need that exists within the soul rather than through eloquent description. Only through such prayer may the soul's bottled-up sorrows be released. With many tears, they dissipate, and in their place, torrents of holy joy rush into the heart.

When a husband sobs for his marriage, it is not a sign of weakness. It demonstrates his mental fortitude and the power God has given him by allowing him to stay married, overcome his weaknesses, and pray for his spouse to turn to God with a sincere heart.

Tears of genuine sympathy of deep affection of children for their parents whose marriage is crumbling are signs of strength, not weakness. And they remain steadfast in their prayers for their parents and other family members. Couples who are sobbing for their marriage are not weak. They typically have minds that are strong and hearts that are strong. It is neither a mere emotional expression of weakness nor a sobbing appearance. It is the outpouring of a powerful soul that is powerful in its love, commitment, and self-sacrifice. If a child of God remains steady during this trial, there are distinctive promises for them:

"When you pass through the waters, I will be with you, and through the rivers, they will not overwhelm you. When you walk through the fire, you will not be burned or scorched, nor will the flame kindle upon you." (Isaiah 43:2).

God's presence is always present among His children. However, if there were ever to be an exception to this rule, it would not apply to people who were distressed, troubled, or sad. The exception would be in the opposite direction.

In a circumstance where a marriage is collapsing, TRUE Christian passion will strive to do the best that sanctified humanity is capable of. As Christians, we are responsible to:

"Remember those who are in prison as if you were their fellow prisoner, and those who are ill-treated, since you also are liable to bodily sufferings." (Hebrews 13:3).

Every time our favorable circumstances cause us to ignore people who are victimized and tortured in their marriages, our own mercies are causing us harm. If one member of the human race, especially one who belongs to the Christian family, suffers, we should all suffer along with them.

"So we, numerous as we are, are one body in Christ (the Messiah) and individually we are parts one of another [mutually dependent on one another]." (Romans 12:5).

Paraclete, The Divorce Lawyer For The Christian

I know a lawyer who has never lost a case in court. He is the "Holy Spirit," the third member of the Trinity. However, during a Christian divorce, I prefer that we refer to Him as OUR PARACLETE. He is a mediator. Thus, He takes neither side. As a mediator in the divorce process between two Christians, the Paraclete acts as a middleman or an intermediary. He steps between the Christian husband and wife who would otherwise be unable to communicate and work to find a solution. It is quite impossible to fully convey the meaning of the Word Paraclete to anyone because it has so many layers.

Paraclete literally means "called to" or "called beside" another person to help them. It shares a verbal similarity, but not a semantic one, with the Latin word, which refers to a representative hired to advocate on our behalf. However, because we now use the word "advocate" in a different context, it would only partially capture the meaning similar to how the word "comforter" does. The word "paraclete" is more expansive than "advocate" and "comforter". The two concepts of "called to" and "calling to" could be used to classify the meaning of the word "paraclete". One summoned to, i.e., to come to our rescue, assist us in our weaknesses, make suggestions, fight for us, lead us, and so on.

Paraclete is someone who, for our benefit, calls and monitors us in situations like abusive marriages and all kinds of relationships so that we can make the best possible decisions. And undoubtedly, the gentle Paraclete is our Guide, Motivator, Reminder, and Comforter in such a difficult situation. His role as one who has been asked to assist us primarily entails strengthening us through moral instruction, teaching, encouragement, and other actions that would fall within the purview of a teacher or a comforter.

Our Paraclete, therefore, states in capital letters that a Christian must flee from the doomed marriage. "Escape; fly from Sodom; 'escape for thy life'" when all attempts to tame a spouse who has long since turned into a lion fail.

The admonition from the angel, who in this context is known as the Paraclete, was to "Escape for your life", not to stop in Sodom and shield Himself from the fire shower under some protective canopy. Therefore, I humbly urge anyone in an abusive marriage or relationship - any violent relationship that causes them to feel despair or puts their precious soul in danger - to escape for their life.

"And when they had brought them forth, they said, Escape for your life! Do not look behind you or stop anywhere in the whole valley; escape to the mountains [of Moab], lest you be consumed" (Genesis 19:17).

If you remain in your current situation, Paraclete cannot offer you any promises of hope, and He cannot offer you any hope in your abusive marriage or any relationship. He says: *"Escape for your life".*

The way I said it - that marriage and eternal life are gifts - might seem incoherent enough to counter the argument on its own. To give eternal life is to give a life that is beyond the pleasures and sorrows of this present mortal life. Even if it were possible, taking it away would not be in line with God's infinite kindness.

However, it is only when we read in the Bible that God divorced Israel that we are able to fully understand how someone might lose their salvation in the same way that someone can lose their marriage. Beloved husbands and wives, the apostasy of Israel and Judah has been written for our instruction.

Certainly, apostasy, just like a divorce, is one of the most terrible things language can describe. It should go without saying that the backslider travels a very dangerous path, both in marriage and salvation.

We are not able to hold our own by human strength. If the precious blood were to lose its virtue, if the good Spirit were to lose His power, or if the right help were to be withheld, we would be without recourse. There is a cure for every kind of sin; trust in Jesus Christ, and you will be saved.

"And *they answered, Believe in the Lord Jesus Christ [give yourself up to Him, take yourself out of your own keeping and entrust yourself into His keeping] and you will be saved, [and this applies both to] you and your household as well."* (Acts 16:31).

There is a cure for every type of marital sin: forgiveness. (Confess your sin to each other). However, there is no cure for apostasy in either marriage or salvation. God will not provide a second sacrifice if someone steps on the first one. He has provided in Jesus Christ. There is only a solitary new birth. Regeneration happens just once.

ESCAPE FOR YOUR LIFE

A struggling or a broken marriage is, in itself, enough to crush a spouse's Spirit and soul. Some spouses put up their best effort to be godly but are not appreciated; instead, they receive abuse and slander. Some people in this world and in the Christian community rejoice at other people's suffering. So, as soon as they learn about someone's marital problems, they immediately exclaim, "Wherever there is smoke, there is always fire;" These individuals fail to remember the adage that "A common liar has common notoriety."; but because they enjoy hearing, speaking and spreading falsehoods, they are certain to believe any fabrication made about a husband and wife.

Such a spouse's souls disintegrate when they hear negative things said about them, especially from people who ought to have inspired them to rise over their troubles. Most husbands and wives who are going through such a terrible situation are tempted to whine: *"I mourn in my complaint and make a noise."* As God's children, it is not welcome to complain about God. However, an abused Christian spouse is far too likely to start believing and complaining that God has abandoned them when their faith is being challenged or when they are subjected to harsh criticism which regularly comes along with marital issues.

Even though Job was the most patient man, he grew quite irritated when his purported "friends" applied acid to his wounds rather than applying the balm. Because of their cruel treatment of him, Job made several remarks that he might have better avoided saying:

"I have heard many such things; wearisome and miserable comforters are you all!" (Job 16:2).

Another prevalent tendency among spouses who are having marital issues is to fully give up and collapse into depression or helplessness as expressed in the following scripture.

"My heart is grievously pained within me, and the terrors of death have fallen upon me." (Psalm 55:4).

When a spouse loses hope, they become apathetic and sit down in a state like a coma; they have no motivation to do anything, not even to pray. Alas, the sudden death of either spouse causes distress in the family, and the one who has murdered ends up in trouble with the law. That is the very true picture of murder that is going on in many families, some of which manifest in the physical.

A well-known gospel artist, whose name I will respectfully withhold, was allegedly killed by her abusive husband. You may be sure that when the late gospel singer was singing, the atmosphere was one of divine inspiration from the Holy Spirit who entered the soul and incited worship by saying: "Worship the Lord."

Although she died a painful death, I am very persuaded that no Christian ever dies untimely. However, I am more disturbed about the several instances in which she passed away while living with such an abusive and a cruel spouse. The abusive death of the late singer and countless others are a metaphor that dissolves with instruction as a beehive dissolves honey, and if they do not teach an abused spouse, it will be their own responsibility.

Every Christian should make the sincerest effort to avoid depression. Just as a Christian should not whine, they should not be depressed also.

Despair, which is the mind's assertion that there is no hope, is more of a sin of the soul than a disorder of the mind. Despair is a serious disrespect to God since it discredits His omnipotence. It is deeply offensive to God's truth. An abused spouse contradicts the Word of God that states: "With God, all things are possible" when they say things like "I am nothing since my marriage is falling apart."

"But Jesus looked at them and said, With men this is impossible, but all things are possible with God" (Matthew 19:26).

It leads people to feel no one loves them; despair is a violation of the promise of God's enduring love for them.

"O GIVE thanks to the Lord, for He is good; for His mercy and loving-kindness endure forever." (Psalm 136:1).

Those who lack hope are likewise devoid of God who is known as "The God of hope."

"May the God of your hope so fill you with all joy and peace in believing [through the experience of your faith] that by the power of the Holy Spirit you may abound and be overflowing (bubbling over) with hope." (Romans 15:13).

There is no legitimate reason for any human to die of despair; if they do, it is a type of suicide and deliberate self-destruction. No Christian has a right to be depressed and can be right while heartbroken. Nobody benefits from despair since it is a bully whose prisons are filled with the corpses of countless dreams as well as those of a medical school, nursing school, law school, and an aviation school certificates.

Despair is a monster that swallows anything that gets in its way. It never did any benefit to the souls it had authority over. In their immense agony, many abused spouses refuse to eat, and occasionally they even reject all forms of comfort. Now, if an abused and a dismayed spouse refuses to eat even when food is put in front of them, they risk starvation and death if they continue to refuse to eat for an extended period of time.

Returning to my previous point about suicide, the abused spouse's cause of death is a suicide, despite the fact that they were innocent. They refused to eat and that may have led to their death. To me, a death brought on by a deliberate refusal to eat does not sound like a natural death.

It sounds like "Taking someone's life away by hunger strike" which is the same as suicide. Suicide of any kind that ends the life of a domestic abuse victim is the same as stabbing oneself in the heart.

CHAPTER 05

THE FAITHFUL HUSBAND IN AN UNFAITHFUL MARRIAGE

Paul says that following the crucifixion of Jesus Christ, God had to dissolve His marriage to Judah in order to be free for both Jesus Christ and the Church to enter into a deeper and better marriage covenant. Thus, the nation of Israel and Judah, all of whom are Jews, is often described as having the characteristics of a married woman. God refers to the Jewish people as His own personal bride, calling Himself the Husband of Israel.

In His revelation to Hosea, God, Himself, confirmed His marriage to be genuine, revealing that He was wed to both Judah and Israel.

Later prophets were inspired by that revelation as they reinterpreted Hosea's words and looked closely at them to further understand God and His relationships with His people. God related with the Jewish in the same way a husband should with his wife. He showered them with all the generosity and tenderness that a husband bestows upon his loving wife. The Jews deemed God as a husband who deserved their devotion, love, and reverence:

"Wives, be subject (be submissive and adapt yourselves) to your own husbands as [a service] to the Lord." "As the church is subject to Christ, so let wives also be subject in everything to their husbands." (Ephesians 5:22 & 24).

God, the Husband, served as a metaphor for the hope and trust of the Jewish people. He provided for the Jewish people in a manner similar to how a wife would expect her Husband to provide for her needs and provide everything she deserves. God was the source of all Jewish hopes and expectations.

Therefore, it is the Husband's responsibility to provide for his wife in every way possible so that she may be satisfied and meet her needs. The nicest aspect is that God was a faithful husband who desired a permanent relationship of love with the Jews.

For a while, God, the true Husband, and His wife, the Jews, were in a committed relationship. They complemented each other well. But unfortunately, God's wife was susceptible to forgetting about Him and His loving kindness and turning to the false gods of the nearby pagan population instead. No one can adequately explain how unfaithful the Jewish people were to the faithful God.

The disobedience of Abraham's descendants to their God was GREAT and terrible. Despite having been selected by a particular favor from among all people and having the great pleasure of hearing God's oracles, they were determined to turn away from God and were unfaithful to their Faithful Husband. The surrounding pagan gods served as a perpetual trap for them, and as a result, they turned away from the One and Only Living True God and bowed down to statues made of wood and stone.

The Jews were never satisfied with one type of idol; they brought new idols from far-off nations like Moab, Egypt, Philistia, Assyria, and the Hittites to worship. The saddest part is that while enjoying God's abundance of temporal comforts, the Jews worshipped their false gods and attributed all those blessings to their false gods. Hear the vile and cruel remarks of the Jewish people:

"I will go after my lovers that give me my food and my water, my wool and my flax, my oil and my refreshing drinks." (Hosea 2:5).

The Jews disregarded God's house's ordinances, or if they were observed externally, they did so in such a callous and a heartless way that their worship insulted God rather than glorifying Him. In countless ways, God lamented over the Jews:

"Why do you gad or wander about so much to change your way? You shall be put to shame by Egypt as you were put to shame by Assyria" (Jeremiah 2:36).

The lamentation ends abruptly and does not seem to make sense on its own. It is an expression of unrequited love. It is a somber lament as God the Husband's affection is focused on His unfaithful wife. The Loving Husband seemed to be telling His wife:

"Even though I have loved you, you are behaving so maliciously toward me. Why do you still wander, then?"

The Bible's portrayal of the Jews as unfaithful spouses who mistreat their spouses and defile themselves in the most heinous ways before divorcing them perfectly represents many modern spouses. When deeply heated with bad passions, they never provide their spouses the love promised to them; instead, they often stray. However, despite their continued disloyalty, their spouses lavishly love them and seek to bring them back home. Many spouses, especially husbands, go astray often because of such bad desires which were never included in the marriage vows. However, just as God, Israel's true spiritual Husband, desired to reunite Israel with Himself out of His abundant love, a wife seeks her Husband's love back to herself through tears and prayer.

God In A Polygamous Marriage!

God is depicted as being married to Israel and Judah in the Old Testament while the church is depicted as the bride of Jesus Christ in the New Testament. In 5712 different places throughout the entire Bible, God and His relationships with the Israelites, Jesus Christ, and the Church are depicted in marriage-related circumstances.

Before anyone uses God's example or my book as a justification for having two marriages, let me clarify that God originally only had one wife. The prophet Jeremiah makes it quite plain that God is married to two sisters, Israel and Judah.

"Return, O faithless children [of the whole twelve tribes], says the Lord, for I am Lord and Master and Husband to you, and I will take you [not as a nation, but individually]—one from a city and two from a tribal family—and I will bring you to Zion" (Jeremiah 3:14).

"And I said, After she has done all these things, she will return to Me; but she did not return, and her faithless and treacherous sister Judah saw it. And I saw, even though [Judah knew] that for this very cause of committing adultery (idolatry) I [the Lord] had put faithless Israel away and given her a bill of divorce; yet her faithless and treacherous sister Judah was not afraid, but she also went and played the harlot [following after idols]. And through the infamy and unseemly frivolity of Israel's whoredom [because her immorality mattered little to her], she polluted and defiled the land, [by her idolatry] committing adultery with [idols of] stones and trees. But in spite of all this, her faithless and treacherous sister Judah did not return to Me in sincerity and with her whole heart, but only in sheer hypocrisy [has she feigned obedience to King Josiah's reforms], says the Lord. And the Lord said to

me, backsliding and faithless Israel has shown herself less guilty than false and treacherous Judah." (Jeremiah 3:7-11).

"Men give gifts to all harlots, but you give your gifts to all your lovers and hire them, bribing [the nations to ally themselves with you], that they may come to you on every side for your harlotries (your idolatrous unfaithfulness to God). And you are different [the reverse] from other women in your harlotries, in that nobody follows you to lure you into harlotry and in that you give hire when no hire is given you; and so you are different." (Ezekiel 16:33-34).

Since the Law of Moses permitted polygamy, the prophets were not bothered to write about this. When Jesus Christ cited: *"... the two will become one flesh" (Matthew 19:5; Mark 10:8)*, He was suggesting that polygamy was not God's original intent. Jesus' statements were a reinterpretation of the Garden of Eden's simple definition of marriage:

"…and they shall become one flesh". (Genesis 2:24).

Despite the fact that it was often added at the end of the paragraph, the word "two" is not included in the Hebrew text. Jesus was joining the expanding Jewish community that accepted the idea that monogamy was the best way to live.

In fact, one can assert that God was a monogamist. God's marriage covenant with Israel and Judah dates back to Mount Sinai before Israel and Judah were separated into separate nations. It follows that God only had one wife to marry. Hosea and Jeremiah point out that the couple's history dates back to the time when Israel left Egypt.

"There I will give her her vineyards and make the Valley of Achor [troubling] to be for her a door of hope and expectation. And she shall

sing there and respond as in the days of her youth and as at the time when she came up out of the land of Egypt" (Hosea 2:15).

"Go and cry in the ears of Jerusalem, saying, Thus says the Lord: I [earnestly] remember the kindness and devotion of your youth, your love after your betrothal [in Egypt] and marriage [at Sinai] when you followed Me in the wilderness, in a land not sown." (Jeremiah 2:2).

The prophet Ezekiel also dates God's marriage to Israel to the time of their arrival in Canaan.

"And say, Thus says the Lord God to Jerusalem [representing Israel]: Your [spiritual] origin and your birth are thoroughly Canaanitish; your [spiritual] father was an Amorite and your [spiritual] mother a Hittite." (Ezekiel 16:3).

Additionally, it should be noted that the prophets' eschatological predictions included the restoration of Israel and Judah as a single nation under a new marriage covenant with her Husband.

"Then shall the children of Judah and the children of Israel be gathered together and appoint themselves one head, and they shall go up out of the land, for great shall be the day of Jezreel [for the spiritually reborn Israel, a divine offspring, the people whom the Lord has blessed." (Hosea 1:11).

"In those days the house of Judah shall walk with the house of Israel, and together they shall come out of the land of the north to the land that I gave as an inheritance to your fathers." (Jeremiah 3:18).

"The word of the Lord came again to me, saying, Son of man, take a stick and write on it, For Judah and the children of Israel his companions; then take another stick and write upon it, For Joseph, the stick of Ephraim, and all the house of Israel his companions;" Ezekiel 37:15-16

God would, thus, be married to only one wife, *as it was in the beginning*. In all circumstances, God upholds His own law according to its letter, but He also works to uphold it according to its spirit. Only He, the God Almighty, is able to marry two wives with the ultimate intention of making them into one. Therefore, in the end, God will marry just one wife after uniting Israel and Judah.

GOD THE DIVORCEE!

We often say that "There is no rule without exception." and it is true that this assertion has an exception of its own because God's laws should be without exception. There is no exception to the rule that God detests divorce

"...I hate divorce and marital separation and him who covers his garment [his wife] with violence" (Malachi 2:16).

There is no exception to God's rule; what God has put together should be no asunder without exception.

"What therefore God has united (joined together), let not man separate or divide." (Mark 10:9).

However, we must never forget that God is severely and rigidly just. If God were not just, He would not be God. He also could not be merciful because Jesus Christ's atoning death — the greatest act of mercy toward the rest of humanity — was also His punishment for sin.

It is truly a horrific thing for a converted soul to ever go from their Savior, just as a converted man's love will wander from a woman in a marriage. God will not divorce His relationship with our souls. Although God and humanity are in a permanent, loving connection, the human soul tries to divorce itself from God. Likewise, a person, who marries their spouse and has enjoyed so much love, yet suddenly begins to mistreat them and abandons them at the end, commits a shameful sin. This is analogous to a redeemed soul who suddenly relapses after receiving so many spiritual benefits from God — including being washed but also clothed, fed, and adopted into the family of God.

Sadly, Israel's repeated infidelity ended her marriage to God in divorce. Judah's marriage to God also experienced a period of many separations as a result of her equally adulterous behavior.

God's unusual instruction to Hosea to marry the harlot Gomer contains the potent themes of marriage forgiveness, an effort for reconciliation, and a promise of a future reunion. He instructed Hosea to marry a woman he was certain would be unfaithful to him and then forgive her. The Jews are portrayed in that representation as an unfaithful wife who seeks to worship other gods and asks Assyria for support, while God is revealed in that representation as the victim of an unfaithful woman.

Although God repeatedly forgave the Jews for their adulterous behavior, it eventually became intolerable and unforgivable. As I previously indicated, God supported Israel as His wife by providing food and clothing, but she rejected this and sought her lovers' support instead. The Jewish people wandered aimlessly without a permanent home for eighteen hundred years, but God never completely abandoned them or violated His covenant with them. God made countless unsuccessful attempts to convince the Jews to return to Him, including using an abundance of love, thunder, a quiet rumbling, pestilence, famine, captivity, and storm.

"Go and proclaim these words toward the north [where the ten tribes have been taken as captives] and say, Return, faithless Israel, says the Lord, and I will not cause My countenance to fall and look in anger upon you, for I am merciful, says the Lord; I will not keep My anger forever" (Jeremiah 3:12).

"Bring charges against your mother, bring charges; For she is not My wife, nor am I her Husband! Let her put away her harlotries from her sight, And her adulteries from between her breasts". (Hosea 2:2).

The immediate impact of His divorcing the Jews was evident because they began to go without the food and clothing their Husband had previously provided, leading to famine and bareness (Hosea 2:3-13).

Ironically, God loved and embraced Judah while He rejected and divorced Israel. (Hoses1:4-8). Judah was still wed to God, but the faithful Husband also provided Israel and a future hope "the day of Jezreel" when Israel and Judah would come together and make peace with God (1:11; 2:14-23), then they would refer to God as "My husband" once they were back together. (2:16).

Isaiah, Jeremiah, and Ezekiel all seem to be interested in God's marriage and His wife's divorce. In his chapters 40–55, the prophet Isaiah returns to this issue in great detail. Isaiah says: "Your Maker is your husband", after inquiring about Judah's divorce proceedings and certificate.

"THUS SAYS the Lord: Where is the bill of your mother's divorce with which I put her away, O Israel? Or which of My creditors is it to whom I have sold you? Behold, for your iniquities you were sold, and for your transgressions was your mother put away" (Isaiah 50:1).

As a result, the prophet declares that God is ready for Judah to return:

"For your Maker is your Husband–the Lord of hosts is His name–and the Holy One of Israel is your Redeemer; the God of the whole earth He is called. For the Lord has called you like a woman forsaken, grieved in spirit, and heartsore–even a wife [wooed and won] in youth, when she is [later] refused and scorned, says your God." (Isaiah 54:5-6).

Jeremiah also made Israel's infidelity with her Husband known.

"Surely, as a wife treacherously and faithlessly departs from her husband, so have you dealt treacherously and faithlessly with Me, O house of Israel, says the Lord." (Jeremiah 3:20).

He instinctively asked whether God would forgive and accept her again after so many adulteries. (Jeremiah 3:1-5). Jeremiah referred to Judah as a young bride.

"Go and cry in the ears of Jerusalem, saying, Thus says the Lord: I [earnestly] remember the kindness and devotion of your youth, your love after your betrothal [in Egypt] and marriage [at Sinai] when you followed Me in the wilderness, in a land not sown." (Jeremiah 2:2).

Judah, however, had emulated her sister Israel's adultery, and God divorced Israel and sent her away with a divorce certificate (Jeremiah 3:6-13). God offered Israel a chance to repent and amend her ways in exchange for the establishment of a new covenant that was not based on the ark of the covenant. At that time, Judah and Israel would once more be unified.

"Return, O faithless children [of the whole twelve tribes], says the Lord, for I am Lord and Master and Husband to you, and I will take you [not as a nation, but individually]–one from a city and two from a tribal

family—and I will bring you to Zion. And I will give you [spiritual] shepherds after My own heart [in the final time], who will feed you with knowledge and understanding and judgment. And it shall be that when you have multiplied and increased in the land in those days, says the Lord, they shall no more say, The ark of the covenant of the Lord. It shall not come to mind, nor shall they [seriously] remember it, nor shall they miss or visit it, nor shall it be repaired or made again [for instead of the ark, which represented God's presence, He will show Himself to be present throughout the city. At that time they shall call Jerusalem The Throne of the Lord, and all the nations shall be gathered to it, in the renown and name of the Lord, to Jerusalem; nor shall they walk any more after the stubbornness of their own evil hearts. In those days the house of Judah shall walk with the house of Israel, and together they shall come out of the land of the north to the land that I gave as an inheritance to your fathers." (Jeremiah 3:14-18).

Ezekiel, the prophet, elaborated on the idea of the two sisters in his twenty-third beginning chapter. He further expounded on the idea that God provided His bride with food and clothing in his sixtieth chapter. Ezekiel mentions the food and clothing provided to Judah, saying that she used them to build or serve gods that were also her lovers and to bribe the countries that were her lovers.

Although divorce and remarriage were expressly permitted by the Law of Moses, the Gospels, as generally understood, seem to forbid both. Within the bounds of the law, remarriage was permitted. Moses in Deuteronomy explicitly stated that a person may remarry, and it even seems to imply that this is true for both the guilty and the innocent spouse.

"When a man takes a wife and marries her, if then she finds no favor in his eyes because he has found some indecency in her, and he writes her a bill of divorce, puts it in her hand, and sends her out of his house, And when she departs out of his house she goes and marries another man," (Deuteronomy 24:1-2)

God is portrayed in both the Old and the New Testaments as someone who submits to His own law about rules governing marriage, separation, divorce, and remarriage.

Now what transpires following God's failed attempts to woo His wife is the key: Divorce and Separation. His marriage with Israel resulted in a divorce while His marriage with Judah endured a period of separation.

CHAPTER 06

THE MYSTERY OF DIVORCE

God's plan for marriage calls for it to be irrevocable. It is like a mystical body, with the husband as the head, the wife as the neck, and the children as the rest of the torso. Now, where are those who attempt to separate the human body's head from its neck? Can the husband be separated from the wife yielding one with himself but not one with his wife? Dreaming of the difficult and paradoxical contradictions of the total and final demise of the entire body makes the faithful husband less distant from his wife than from the entirety of his own loyalty.

Those who have never fully digested the contemplation of a lovely union of marriage will not understand the analogy being depicted here. With the human torso viewed as a component of the body and the spouse serving as the head, how can anyone understand the possibility of dissolution? Can someone successfully relate to body parts? Can they picture someone with a split torso and head having the ideal body?

The finest joints in this magical body of marriage are nonetheless susceptible to strains. They may experience some challenging and risky luxation, but just as with the natural human body which may be involved in a serious accident but not have a single bone broken due to an all-powerful Providence when it is most vulnerable to all adversaries' brutality in death, so it is with God-centered marriages.

The mystical marriage might endure some beatings and blows. If a husband, a wife, or a child were left alone, there might be occasional bumps and cuts, but no bone should be broken in pieces, much less detached from the rest of the body. Or could any of them be even slightly separated from the body from which they are to be. They are susceptible to the same heinous flaws and perilous and fatal miscarriages.

However, because it pleased the Father God to join them, it is now important for them to preserve their integrity to uphold the honor of the mystical marriage body.

Christians should respect the earthly marriage in the same way they accept their devoted soul as wedded in truth and righteousness to Jesus Christ, the heavenly husband. There should not be any divorce lawsuits filed here on Earth, just as no one can imagine any having been filed in Heaven.

Can anyone imagine that what was done in the earthly paradise, as an example, would actually be undone in the heavenly? Does anyone really believe that the immutable God has second thoughts? What an Infinite Power has put together, can they imagine that a limited power can disjoin.

"And Pharisees came to Him and put Him to the test by asking, Is it lawful and right to dismiss and repudiate and divorce one's wife for any and every cause?" (Matthew 19:3).

Whenever the Pharisees try to tempt Jesus Christ, He does what He does best: He makes them think they are clever when they are not. In this scenario, He drew His interrogators' attention to the founding institution of marriage and declared:

"So they are no longer two, but one flesh. What therefore God has joined together, let not man put asunder (separate)" (Matthew 19:6).

There is no restriction against separating those whom God has not joined. Whom exactly has He joined together? In the first marital institution, God's opinion is:

"Now the Lord God said, It is not good (sufficient, satisfactory) that the man should be alone; I will make him a helper (suitable, adapted, complementary) for him" (Genesis 2:18).

God alone may join in what He intended and what He promised. In matrimony, Apostle Paul says: *"God has called us to peace."*

"But if the unbelieving partner [actually] leaves, let him do so; in such [cases the remaining] brother or sister is not morally bound. But God has called us to peace" (1 Corinthians 7:15).

God joins a man and a woman when He invites them to marriage. Never does God violate any of His own commands. However, not every marriage is the union of God. He doesn't decide which exact man and which specific woman we should get married to. Any rational individual will not accept the idea that God is the one who has joined every union that society now refers to as marriage. It is possible for a man and a woman to get married entirely out of their own passion without the involvement of God. God does not approve of a young lady who marries a billion for his money or status: "Amor nummi. Auri sacra fames. Caveat emptor!"

"For the love of money is a root of all evils; it is through this craving that some have been led astray and have wandered from the faith and pierced themselves through with many acute [mental] pangs." (1 Timothy 6:10).

Incest, zoophilia (the marriage of humans and animals), same-sex marriages, and other relationships of this nature are not approved nor joined by God because they never enter into the mystical marriage between Jesus Christ and His Holy Church which is symbolized by the estate of holy matrimony. Such unions are not arranged honestly and in fear of God, but rather, otherwise, than what God's word does permit. Thus, God made irrevocability a part of the basic structure of His divinely appointed marriage. It continued as a common practice among all nations for a very long period. The Greeks of Homer's Day don't appear to have known what divorce was. Divorce does not seem to have been something that the Greeks of Homer's Day were familiar with. In contrast, many other nations swiftly abandoned the idea of irrevocability.

The idea of irrevocability has now been quickly forgotten in many nations for a variety of reasons. God's commandment through Moses does not appear to have been highly appreciated by anyone and is not enforced very seriously.

No non-Christian country today hardly acknowledges irrevocability. The Christian nations that pride themselves in having made the most advancement in civilization are losing ground to it. The United States, a country whose Founding Fathers frequently cited the Bible and credited it for the success of the country, does not acknowledge the irrevocability of marriage.

The importance of God's decree that marriage be irrevocable must be emphasized to the world even more. Irrevocable denotes more than just permanence. Permanence just suggests that the entity being examined will survive under normal conditions, not that it can never run its course.

In general, the term "irrevocable" implies to something that cannot be ended or dissolved.

The marriage bond is inseparable in the sense that God created it and should only be dissolved with His permission. No human authority should be able to dissolve it. This and the fact that there may be a specific circumstance in which the Divine Law permits the dissolution of a marriage are not inconsistent.

How To Overcome Evils Relating To Divorcing

The idea that marriage is irrevocably bound together has fallen out of favor. This can be explained simply. Evils can be defeated in a number of ways; however, for the sake of this book, I will focus on three. The first, which is deserving of the title "Christian proverb" and which is presented in a way that is highly useful for memory is "Overcome evil with Good", which is "Godlike". The second way to stop evil from happening is by making people experience their repercussions which is "Human-like". The option is to lessen their effects at the risk of seeing more instances which is both "Godlike and "Human-like." The first and second examine the overall decline of evil. The last considers the consolation of unfortunate victims. Both the first two and a part of the final appear divine. And a portion of the final form is solely human.

Punishment, Whether Divine Or Human, Are Corrective In Nature (God-like)

God allows suffering to accompany wrongdoing. Humans merely attempt to alleviate suffering. The laws that govern the world put greater punishments on crime as a natural consequence rather than only as a legal criminal punishment. The behaviors of the sufferer invariably result in their suffering, sometimes leading to behaviors that people recognize as terrible; other times, leading to actions that people simply regard as idiotic or ignorant. Even when it arises from wrongdoing, it usually bears a proportion to it because that is incredibly stunning to most men regardless of whether it results from recklessness, carelessness, or disobedience.

Sometimes, even behaviors that would hardly qualify as ill-advised cause disease and death. Because the first Adam stood as the federal head and representation of the entire human race, we were all susceptible to the terrible effects of his fall. It is clear from human experiences that God regarded Adam as the patriarch and head of his natural descendants under the covenant of works. Therefore, when he fell, we also fell in him and were vulnerable to the terrible effects of his fall. Death, condemnation, and judgment entered the world as a result of Adam's fall. Those are all God's laws which humans mistakenly refer to be laws of nature, but which God actually ordained.

It is insufficient to casually assert that they have been appointed for good intentions as some men occasionally do. They must also be chosen for wise and good reasons that man is totally unable to understand. While such laws appear to man to solely cause evil, God recognizes that they also produce good.

The entire universe, everything in it, and all of their connections and relationships over time, are all simultaneously visible to God. Man is limited to a partial and lopsided vision of a very small number of objects and to a very limited understanding of their relationships with one another. However, we have no understanding whatsoever of their relationships with the whole. Even though we may kill sentient people in our path, we are unable to understand the rigidity of nature's laws or the consistency with which effects follow their causes. However, it is possible to respectfully speculate that one of God's goals in designing those laws was to teach people to be mindful of their conduct.

Irrevocability Is Embedded In The Law

The Divine law which forbids termination of a marriage once it has been established is comparable to the physical laws that have just been discussed. It focuses on people who engage in marriage and the effects of their inevitable decision. It so cautions people to be cautious about how and with whom they develop close and irretrievable relationships.

Sadly, many people do not even open their first spelling book or go over the ABCs of marriage before getting married, so they do not know that:

"…they are no longer two, but one flesh. What therefore God has joined together, let not man put asunder (separate)" (Matthew 19:6).

Many people lack basic knowledge or have forgotten the alphabet of marriage. Therefore, they marry for the wrong reasons, and some marry impulsively not knowing the people to whom they pledge their happiness and comfort in this life and possibly in the next. Therefore, they date and get married to people who are unfit to be their husbands or wives.

The natural laws run their predetermined course. Constant disagreement leads to abuse of all forms and misery. Nothing, not even the termination of the marriage, can stop or reverse the evil. However, it is theorized that in some circumstances, a separation and a careful review of the ABCs of marriage can moderate such marital chaos.

Man Set The Law Of Divorce To Appease Their Feelings (Human-Like)

Humans are often driven to stop suffering, especially in circumstances that directly impact their feelings and thoughts since they only see things in the context of the situation. We are limited, and when we attempt to imagine perfection - without a single flaw or mistake - we fail because we are flawed. We are, therefore, unable to recognize or understand how anything is related to the totality, just as the finite cannot understand the infinite.

We would never enforce a strict law because we would be motivated by the pain of particular people rather than be able to grasp how the rule would benefit us. We would never have ruled that a marriage should be irrevocable. We observe the negative effects of unsuitable marriages in specific situations, and in each instance, we want to bring relief to the victims. We are unable to observe how the strict rule affects the overall level of happiness in the world because measuring it is beyond the scope of human intelligence.

Both men and women experience the effects of their own remorseful recklessness. They sincerely want relief, and other people also want to alleviate them.

Empathy for the suffering is never satisfied to play a single role. Any person in a position of leadership who is distraught over a spouse who is being mistreated in their marriage would surely invite others to express their sentiments.

They find it so unbearable that they wish other people would begin to feel sorry for the abused. Such sympathizers whose anguish seems to be so severe if they are to work with the parliament or congress, hang the miseries of the abuse on the sky in darkness and cover the earth in sackcloth. Due to their empathy for those who have been abused in marriages, human legislators propose and enact legislation allowing for the termination of marriages.

Conflict Of Interest Of Human Law And Divine Law

If lawmakers were to be a little more open-minded and truthful about how they feel about the divorce laws they pass, they would likely admit that they either violate their consciences or consciously reject the Divine institution of marriage while justifying their actions with human knowledge and experience. However, we must take care not to see their mistakes as justifications because doing so has resulted in the infusion of poisons rather than beneficial fluids into the marriage institution.

Due to the high number of unhappy marriages, many Legislators have concluded that unsuitable marriages should be terminated. It is true that many spouses have a distorted perception of marriage. They are hardly the type of people one would expect to find in depicting a God-ordained marriage.

Some people who slyly slip into marriage are a menace to their spouses and to the society. They display the rage and fury of a brute. The worst kind of brute is one that is human. No creature is as savage as the beast in man, nor the wolf, tiger, or snake. They harm themselves and other people when they are angry. Such people require chaining, supervision, and general protection from other people and marriage.

People who have love for both themselves and others should be married. People who do not want to hurt other people are unlikely to harm themselves. Some people are godly, sober, consistent, honest, and kind. There would be points of disagreement between a husband and a wife, which would render it impossible for them to be of any service to each other or for anything that they do to be of any value to the family, church, and state.

In many of those scenarios, the husband - whether or not he is at fault - should assume the position of Jesus Christ who formulates methods to make peace with the sinner through Himself. When God refers to Himself as "God, and not man", He specifically notes that He is superior to and more forgiving than man because of His greater grace, patience, and longsuffering:

"I will not execute the fierceness of My anger; I will not bring back Ephraim to nothing or again destroy him. For I am God and not man, the Holy One in the midst of you, and I will not come in wrath or enter into the city" (Hosea 11:9)

In a million ways, a husband should be more influential than a woman when it comes to resolving family disputes. Unfortunately, due to the narrowness and shallowness of their goodwill, many spouses have failed to fulfill their obligations which have resulted in lawmakers' unknowingly performing sympathizing service and man-pleaser duties to pass divorce laws. However, if they were sincere, they would acknowledge that they are unsure of the number of unhappy marriages that the irrevocableness rule's use of caution has avoided. Or, more precisely, how many would be prevented if the rule was not violated? Even if they do, they still will not be able to find the right balance because no human mind can simultaneously process and compare all the details.

Since it is not impossible to learn everything there is to know about marriage and its irrevocability, all human thinking must be flawed. Even if they could, they would be too many and complex for the human mind to process.

We have no choice but to rely on the divine knowledge revealed in the Bible. Immoral laws are passed because modern lawmakers prioritize their own. However, it is vital to note that anyone who claims to receive God's revelation must do so confidently and abide by God's laws of government. No matter what condition mankind finds themselves in, the timeless truth is that marriage is irrevocable and is between a man and a woman according to God's revealed Will. That is the book's main premise. There will be times when nothing more is necessary than returning to the premise. The writings are, thus, quite similar to those that have been used to prove that God has institutionalized marriage.

POSSIBLE ORIGIN OF DIVORCE

The children of God in the time of the prophets, judges, and Jesus Christ were the same as the true child of God today. There is, without a doubt, a decline in moral character as we approach the "LAST DAYS" of Jesus Christ. But the depth of a child of God's knowledge about God shapes their character.

The life that a Christian will lead in Heaven is given to them through rebirth here on earth. A child of God is born for Heaven when they are reborn. They, thereafter, receive the life that endures throughout the eras of eternity.

Now, when we consider the beginning of marriage, we read about Adam and Eve, then Cain and Awan. In the years that followed, we read about Abraham and Sarah, Isaac and Rebecca, and Jacob, Rachelle and Leah. We, also, read about Moses and Zipporah. Still further back, until the period of the judges, kings, and prophets, up until Joseph, the purported Father of Jesus and Mary, His mother, we read about marriage.

Given the longevity of marriages, it is likely that believers have always understood God's intended meaning of marriage's irrevocability. For a very long time, people believed that marriage was irrevocable. There are no references to divorce anywhere in the entire Book of Genesis. Abraham and Isaac disguised their wives as their sisters in order to escape being slain by those who could be attracted to Sarah and Rebecca respectively. It does not appear that Abraham and Isaac thought about the possibility that the kings of the Gentiles could demand that they divorce their wives. Because the examples of polygamy described in the Bible are all so egregiously wrong, there is no need for the practice to be condemned in such strong terms because even in its mildest forms, polygamy is inherently evil. In Jacob's case, it worked startlingly well. I worry that his devoted wife, Rachel, is to blame for the family's introduction of teraph, or symbol worship, a type of idolatry. Rachel had acquired it from her Father, Laban, and had practiced it privately. Despite being almost aware of it, Jacob did not want to speak to her, his sweetheart and the ruler of his soul.

Maybe Jacob did not want to dim the bright eyes which had charmed him years ago with tears. Perhaps Jacob did not want to ruin with tears of the beautiful eyes that had enchanted him years earlier. Conflict arose as the sons of Leah advocated their mother's cause while the handmaids' sons took sides with one another.

Because there were so many mothers in the family, it was difficult to organize and maintain a functioning household. It was not what a family of believers should be, so it is not surprising that things went so horribly wrong that it seemed salt was losing its flavor and the good seed was dying before it could be planted in the ground and made to bear fruit.

There was a necessity to take a position. There was a duty to be fulfilled, and Jacob must fulfill it. God stepped in and spoke with Jacob; because Jacob had a good heart toward God's laws, God simply needed to speak to him to get his attention in order to obey Him. God called Jacob to a halt, forced him to take stock of the situation, and ordered his household affairs. He did that with the same resolve of character that was only apparent when Jacob was placed in a difficult situation. Jacob did not appear to have thought about divorcing any of his wives even during such turmoil.

Soon after the Exodus, the Israelites began to practice divorce; it was possible that they learned the practice in Egypt. The knowledge of countries was rather limited at the time. But in relation to Israel, Egypt occupies a rather unique position. It is frequently regarded as the haven of the progeny of Abraham. When there was a famine in the country where he was sojourning, Abraham himself went there.

In order to avoid the death that his jealous brothers had planned for him and to become the foster Father of the house of Israel, God allowed Joseph to be sold to Egypt. Jacob's entire family traveled to Egypt at Joseph's invitation. There they stayed in a foreign country. Egypt, which had once provided protection for the House of Israel, later changed into a haven for slaves and a place where the chosen people's very lives were in jeopardy.

The children of Israel were people whom God had chosen. He was determined to make them a powerful nation and a remarkable people so that He could teach them the law and the testimony. God had a very good reason for allowing Joseph to travel to Egypt first, was then followed by Jacob and the rest of the family. He intended for the Israelites to unite as a nation and learn many practical skills they would not have been able to gain while they were dispersed over Palestine. The lesson was priceless, but it was acquired through great suffering.

After settling in Egypt for a while, Jacob's family and their progeny were content there. The Egyptian pharaoh showed the Israelites a lot of favor. And in Goshen, where Joseph's parents and siblings lived, the soil also yielded copiously. Israel was great and prosperous. Therefore, the majority of Israelites had little intention of ever leaving Egypt. They made the decision to stay there forever.

Some Israelites attempted to blend into Egyptian society, despite God's will that it ought not to be so. They started to forget their distinct heritage because they were a part of the Egyptian people. And most likely, if left to their own devices, they would have melted and assimilated into the Egyptian race.

The Israelites would no longer have been recognized as God's chosen people. They were happy to be in Egypt and were open to becoming Egyptianized. They started to emulate Egypt's sorcery, idolatry, and sins to a significant extent. And in the years that followed, those things stuck to them to such a dreadful degree that it can easily be assumed that their hearts must have gone away greatly in favor of Egypt's sins.

However, God remained steadfast in His resolve to freeing them from their wicked relationship. He would not let the Israelites be Egyptians or continue to live permanently as Egyptians. He must separate them. God had chosen them out. He also intended to draw a permanent distinction between Egypt and Israel. God had to make Israel hate Egypt in order to free them from the country.

Joseph, who rose to become a prime minister, enjoyed widespread favor in Egypt. Every Egyptian still respected the Israelites in memory of him even after his passing. They might have continued to live comfortably in Egypt. Israel would not have left Egypt of her own volition if she had not been forcibly expelled.

They had the desire not to leave the fatty Nile Delta, for all went well with them. Instead, they behaved like sheep in clover and loved their deep grazing like a bullock. God made the Israelites hate Egypt in anticipation of their liberation. So, a new ruler who was unfamiliar with Joseph emerged.

"Now a new king arose over Egypt who did not know Joseph" (Exodus 1:8).

He was a king who believed that the presence of a foreign population within his country was dangerous. He must start by, if at all possible, reducing their numbers. The King forced the Israelites to work for him and perform slave labor for free. The Israelites kept growing, even under extremely hard work. Therefore, the Egyptian king ensured the Israelites did not receive straws and had to obtain their own straw to construct the bricks.

"The very same day Pharaoh commanded the taskmasters of the people and their officers, You shall no more give the people straw to make brick; let them go and gather straw for themselves" (Exodus 5:6-7).

When they complained of no straw, they were told to provide double the number of bricks, which caused them to sigh, sob, and grumble because of their taskmasters.

"Then the Hebrew foremen came to Pharaoh and cried, Why do you deal like this with your servants?" (Exodus 5:15)

The iron bondage invaded Israel's soul, causing him to hurt under the flogging and faint under strain. As a result, the Israelites wailed sending a piercing cry to the heavens.

"Now behold, the cry of the Israelites has come to Me, and I have also seen how the Egyptians oppress them" (Exodus 3:9)

The advent of freedom coincided with the time when the greatest burdens were placed upon them. When the brick task had doubled for the Israelites, Moses was born in Egypt. In a fortuitous act, God gave Moses access to all the knowledge in Egypt that would later be crucial to the freedom of the Israelites. Moses was educated in all that Egypt had to offer and was raised in some of the finest schools of the day, but he never allowed his faith in God to waver.

Moses, an Israelite, in fact, refused to hide his heritage or give it up by naturalizing as an Egyptian. He kept his ground, even if it meant breaking his foster mother's heart and facing death. Moses murdered an Egyptian and fled for forty years.

"One day, after Moses was grown, it happened that he went out to his brethren and looked at their burdens; and he saw an Egyptian beating a Hebrew, one of [Moses'] brethren. He looked this way and that way, and when he saw no one, he killed the Egyptian and hid him in the sand" (Exodus 2:11-12).

The Israelites were scattered among the nations, but when the time was right, God sent Moses to Egypt to gather them all and form a distinct people for Himself. God intended for them to have an inheritance, even the land of milk and honey so that they may live there as witnesses to His covenant and uphold His commandments.

"And I have declared that I will bring you up out of the affliction of Egypt to the land of the Canaanite, the Hittite, the Amorite, the Perizzite, the Hivite, and the Jebusite, to a land flowing with milk and honey" (Exodus 3:17).

However, Israel's slavery in Egypt was a dismal one. They could not be freed by human effort alone unless God intervened and performed miracles on their behalf.

So, through Moses, God brought about plague after plague until Pharaoh eventually released the Israelites.

"Then the Lord said to Moses, Go to Pharaoh and tell him, Thus says the Lord God of the Hebrews: Let My people go, that they may serve Me" (Exodus 9:1).

The very minimum calculations indicate that there must have been 2.5 million Israelites who left Egypt. They all gathered in one location and left the nation at the same time. In addition to that, a mixed multitude made up of a very large group of people also left with them. It is difficult to imagine the number which must have been quite high. Those Egyptians were not part of the children of Israel although traveling with them. Despite their successful escape, the door was only opened to let the children of Israel depart.

It is reported that the mixed multitude became enamored. And it was the mixed multitude who persuaded the Israelites to worship the golden calf. The different populations easily deceived them, who may have even encouraged them to think that divorce was acceptable.

Those diverse individuals now have representatives. Many join our church fellowship, partake of the communion bread, and drink from the communion cup, yet they are not one of us, much like how many people left Egypt but were never Israelites. Among many other things, they and others like them are preaching divorce to God's real children. They were never held in servitude in Egypt; they were a mixed multitude. Israel was the one who had to endure the taskmaster's lash and create the bricks without the use of a straw.

However, those people did not suffer alongside them. They were Egyptians in their own right - true Egyptians.

"...We were then by nature children of [God's] wrath and heirs of [His] indignation, like the rest of mankind" (Ephesians 2:3).

They never experienced true servitude; therefore, they were unable to understand what it meant to be set free from sin.

GOD HATES DIVORCE

A lack of knowledge of God's law is the source of many sins. In this usage, the word "law" refers to the fullness of biblical revelation from God. It is not only the law of the Ten Commandments but the entire Sacred Book. The Bible contains God's thoughts to the extent that He has decided to reveal them to humans.

There have been some extremely grave mistakes made regarding the law of God. Some Christians claim that the law has been completely abolished and annulled. They publicly propagate the idea that Christians are not required to live according to the moral law. They regard what would have been sin in other men to be no sin in themselves. Although the law is not the means of our salvation, we should be pleased to see it in the hands of Jesus Christ and ready to follow them in everything.

Many believe that Jesus Christ tempered and moderated the law. They have effectively claimed that since imperfect beings could not obey God's perfect law, God has, instead, provided us with a softer law.

"For truly I tell you, until the sky and earth pass away and perish, not one smallest letter nor one little hook [identifying certain Hebrew letters] will pass from the Law until all things [it foreshadows] are accomplished" (Matthew 5:18).

Such people walk dangerously close to making awful mistakes though it is doubtful they are fully conscious of it. And great sin usually begins with little sins.

The Bible contains the law of the heavenly kingdom and the law of eternal life in Christ Jesus. The Bible convinces us that the law of works governs sin. And as a law of love, it directs us to Jesus Christ who died on the cross to atone for our sins.

The law of faith is the means by which we receive His grace, and the law of holiness serves as our standard for behavior. And a Christian who understands the relative positions of the law and the gospel can triumph from a doctrine perspective in the circumstance. Every Christian needs to be aware of two things: how the law relates to them and how it condemns them, and how the gospel relates to them and how it justifies them if they are Christians. The law is the same today as it was in Malachi's day. Godly people are to hold on to whatever God has revealed.

With reference to Adam's remarks in Eden when God first introduced a woman to him, Malachi makes an insightful marriage-related statement. He says:

"Yet you ask, why does He reject it? Because the Lord was witness [to the covenant made at your marriage] between you and the wife of your youth, against whom you have dealt treacherously and to whom you were faithless. Yet she is your companion and the wife of your covenant [made by your marriage vows]. And did not God make [you and your wife] one [flesh]? Did not One make you and preserve your

spirit alive? And why [did God make you two] one? Because He sought a godly offspring [from your union]. Therefore, take heed to yourselves, and let no one deal treacherously and be faithless to the wife of his youth. For the Lord, the God of Israel, says: I hate divorce and marital separation and him who covers his garment [his wife] with violence. Therefore, watch your spirit [that My Spirit may control it] and deal not treacherously and faithlessly [with your marriage mate]. You have wearied the Lord with your words. Yet you say, in what way have we wearied Him? [You do it when by your actions] you say, everyone who does evil is good in the sight of the Lord, and He delights in them. Or [by asking], Where is the God of justice?" (Malachi 2:14-17).

Malachi quotes God as saying categorically affirming everything above. There is a connection between the creation of just one woman and the oneness of the flesh, which Adam said existed between himself and his wife. Thus, Adam impliedly foretold or commanded that such would be between all future men and their wives.

The paragraph before appears to have been a conversation. In it, the prophet poses as though he is being questioned and then gives arguments that imply putting away a spouse is to act treacherously:

"Yet you ask, why does He reject it? Because the Lord was witness [to the covenant made at your marriage] between you and the wife of your youth, against whom you have dealt treacherously and to whom you were faithless. Yet she is your companion and the wife of your covenant [made by your marriage vows]" (Malachi 2:14).

It is legitimate for anyone to inquire about Judah's purported treachery. The answers are practical: profaning the holiness of God, whom he adored, by marrying the daughter of a different god. This was supposedly a method of speaking about idolatry.

After the captivity, however, idolatry did not become widespread among Jews. They would not have asked the prophet why he accused them of idolatry if they were accustomed to doing it. The Israelites committed sins that went beyond simply marrying a foreign god's daughter. Their offenses included cruelty, abuse, etc. It covered God's altar with tears, with weeping, and with crying out.

"And this you do with double guilt; you cover the altar of the Lord with tears [shed by your unoffending wives, divorced by you that you might take heathen wives], and with [your own] weeping and crying out because the Lord does not regard your offering any more or accept it with favor at your hand" (Malachi 2:13).

The altar was not for the foreign God but for the God of Israel. The height of their cruelty was not human sacrifices although it was unusual at the time. The Israelites committed a crime that included treachery: "Judah hath dealt treacherously." Following those assertions, the prophet introduces the Jews as inquiring, "Wherefore?" This could imply: Why do you make such unfounded accusations against us? Otherwise, why wouldn't God accept our offering or recognize that we made it? The reason is that:

"Yet you ask, Why does He reject it? Because the Lord was witness [to the covenant made at your marriage] between you and the wife of your youth, against whom you have dealt treacherously and to whom you were faithless. Yet she is your companion and the wife of your covenant [made by your marriage vows]" (Malachi 2:14).

The explanation for the treachery is given as follows: You have forsaken the woman who is regarded as your wife from your youth, *"She is your companion and the wife of your covenant [made by your marriage vows]"*. Whatever the specific purpose of the question, it is evident that if he divorces his wife, God will not accept his offering. The Old Testament ends its discussion of marriage with this evidence of its irrevocable nature.

A Flimsy Excuse

Many Christians who secretly want a justification to divorce their spouse have taken seriously Moses' command that the Israelites send the woman away and produce a divorce certificate. But if the Israelites' conduct is properly understood, their mental state justifies the description of *"A Document of Divorce"*.

In His Sermon on the Mount, Jesus Christ affirms:

"It hath been said, Whosoever shall put away his wife, let him give her writing of divorcement; but I say unto you, that whosoever shall put away his wife, saving for the cause of fornication, causes her to commit adultery, and whosoever shall marry her that is divorced committeth adultery." (Matthew 5:31-32 KJV).

Jesus, on another occasion, pointed the Pharisees' attention to Genesis in response to their question about divorce:

"And Pharisees came to Him and put Him to the test by asking, Is it lawful and right to dismiss and repudiate and divorce one's wife for any and every cause?" (Matthew 19:3).

He used the beginning of marriage as a model to give them the right response.

"So God created man in His own image, in the image and likeness of God He created him; male and female He created them" (Genesis 1:27).

"Therefore a man shall leave his father and his mother and shall become united and cleave to his wife, and they shall become one flesh" (Genesis 2:24).

Then Jesus explained the two verses in His own divine commentary:

"So they are no longer two, but one flesh. What therefore God has joined together, let not man put asunder (separate)" (Matthew 19:6).

Jesus Christ implied that the husband who puts his wife out would force her to commit adultery based on where he stood on divorce. But how should the words be interpreted? The husband does not physically coerce or even recommend that the wife should have an affair with another man. When asked, Jesus Christ is never reluctant to provide a spiritual explanation for what He says. The Jews did not immediately recognize the spiritual implications of His analogies and sayings. And practically all of their disagreements with Him arose from that.

So, on adultery, Jesus Christ addressed it in more detail, highlighting its spiritual nature. The Jews thought that the command "You shall not kill" simply forbade murder and manslaughter: but Jesus Christ showed that anger without cause violates the law. He explained that the commandment forbade hard words, cursing, and all other displays of enmity and malice. The Pharisees knew that they might not commit adultery, but it did not enter into their minds that a lascivious desire would be an offense against the precept till Jesus said:

"But I say to you that everyone who so much as looks at a woman with evil desire for her has already committed adultery with her in his heart" (Matthew 5:28).

He demonstrated that the thinking of evil is sin, that an impure imagination pollutes the heart, and that a rash wish is a sin in the eyes of God. Jesus would have surely made reference to Moses' order to the Israelites to issue a "Certificate of Divorce" if it were a proper response to the Pharisees' query. However, it is clear from Jesus' response to their argument that Moses' commands did not fully respond to their concern regarding the appropriateness of divorce. He disregarded the command by contesting the directive's relevance to the divorce-related question. The law of the Mosaic period which recognized divorce as a reality in Israelite society was a reflection of the Israelite's stony hearts. The rules of the day which acknowledged divorce as a reality in Israelite society, were shaped by the people's hard hearts.

Egypt clearly influenced the first two generations of Israelites, as I have undoubtedly already stated. A permissive attitude toward divorce was probably a result of Egypt's impact establishing a custom that existed even before God made His covenant at Sinai.

In no way did that acknowledgment imply a divine endorsement or support of divorce. The law neither made divorce mandatory nor made it a legal right. Those who make divorce their hobby commit heinous sins; they act of their own free will, and they bear full responsibility for their actions. Since human beings have free will, this is the truth that no one can ever forget. Now, the complicated topic of "the will" has been the focal point of the key argument that has split the Christian Church for many ages. Humans' "Will" has its proper place in their behavior.

The Bible, in so many instances, addresses humans as a being having a will. And since God made us in His image and likeness, it implies that God has a "Will". And because of the nature of God, His "Will" is immutable.

The Bible has no discourse on the worth of human nature or the beauty of human character. But only God is holy, and when He looks down from Heaven, He finds not even one person doing good.

"As it is written, None is righteous, just and truthful and upright and conscientious, no, not one" (Romans 3:10).

Humanity and our "will" pale in comparison to God's will which is flawless in every way. From Abraham to Malachi, God's will is all-powerful. God is omnipotent, and He works out His wise designs. Very little consideration is given in the Bible to any fancied rights and claims of humans. The concept that the all-powerful Creator would take notice of humanity is, therefore, astounding.

Contrary to what people would want to believe, people do not ultimately control world events. No matter how powerful we might think we are, we have supreme authority. Whatever men may want or decide to do, there is a Power that governs, overrules, and acts in accordance with Its own benevolent will - as God did in the past, amid the fury of human anger, the tempest of human sin, and even in the deepest dungeons of human ambition and oppression. Just as the potter shapes the objects on the wheel according to His will, God continually manifests His sovereign will among humans.

A Dead Conscience Sees Nothing Wrong With Sin

Most people do not take sin seriously unless it brings them within the jurisdiction of the law of the land. They laugh at it as if it were a trifle; but God does not think of sin as humans do. God condemns sin in extremely severe language and characterizes it by highly derogatory names. God knows what sin is. He does not think it is trivial since He can judge it better than we can. God refers to a man or a woman who divorces and remarries as engaging in "adultery". The scripture below supports that:

"It has also been said, Whoever divorces his wife must give her a certificate of divorce. But I tell you, Whoever dismisses and repudiates and divorces his wife, except on the grounds of unfaithfulness (sexual immorality), causes her to commit adultery, and whoever marries a woman who has been divorced commits adultery". (Matthew 5:31-32).

To many people, adultery does not appear to be a sin. In our natural state, humans are spiritually blind and ignorant of what sin is. The God of this world has blinded those who do not believe. So, it is incredibly dangerous to deny that Jesus is the Son of God.

The fall of Adam is what led to spiritual blindness. And we gain sight through the new birth of Jesus Christ. Even though a person may be a skilled entrepreneur, a scientist, a philosopher, or a politician, if they are without Jesus Christ, they are spiritually blind. Even worse, if Christians continue to knowingly break God's law, they risk losing their spiritual sight. Despite losing their spiritual vision, people may still be well-versed in the scriptures regarding what God forbids.

However, they develop a defensive response to the same instruction they might have readily accepted. They suddenly start to argue and justify why that biblical scripture is no longer rational. When Christians have a terrible perverted misunderstanding about anything and remain satisfied with this misconception, their actions turn evil. And in cases that are being looked into because of a hardened heart, the spouse who has decided to file for divorce no longer hears the voice of their conscience.

Like the banished king Saul, they start to feel restless, and so, they turn to music to calm their rebellious spirits. If the music fails, they request Nabal's feast. At the feast, sheep are shorn, and the would-be divorcee consumes wine till their souls are so inebriated that their stoicism is as stone-like. Maybe when the music and wine run out, they also call for the dance, and the daughter of Herodias asks Herod for the head of John the Baptist to pay the dance's fatal price. And yet, they are still at peace. Any person would undoubtedly feel at peace if their heart were that stone-hard. They stare at their consciences, and they are surprised when they don't feel anything.

Well, if a prospective Christian divorcee moves from one of those scenarios to another, I have no trouble answering the difficult question:

"And I thought how [gloriously and honorably] I would set you among My children and give you a pleasant land, a goodly heritage, the most beautiful and best [inheritance] among all nations! And I thought you would call Me My Father and would not turn away from following Me." (Jeremiah 3:19).

Ultimately, they defy all advice and have their marriage dissolved by the state. In spite of their attempts to appease an obstinate conscience for a while, their sin of adultery continues to drag them down to hell even as its notes lift them up to heaven. These are the principal, if not all, texts to support the above discourse.

"But to the married people I give charge - not I but the Lord - that the wife is not to separate from her husband. But if she does [separate from and divorce him], let her remain single or else be reconciled to her husband. And [I charge] the husband [also] that he should not put away or divorce his wife" (1 Corinthians 7:10-11).

"Husbands, love your wives, as Christ loved the church and gave Himself up for her. So that He might sanctify her, having cleansed her by the washing of water with the Word. That He might present the church to Himself in glorious splendor, without spot or wrinkle or any such things [that she might be holy and faultless]. Even so husbands should love their wives as [being in a sense] their own bodies. He who loves his own wife loves himself. For no man ever hated his own flesh, but nourishes and carefully protects and cherishes it, as Christ does the church. Because we are members (parts) of His body. For this reason a man shall leave his father and his mother and shall be joined to his wife, and the two shall become one flesh. This mystery is very great, but I speak concerning [the relation of] Christ and the church" (Ephesians 5:25-32).

SEPARATION IS AS SINFUL AS DIVORCE

As I mentioned earlier, the Bible does not always provide a particular rule to address every possible type of moral emergency. In God's eyes, the position of a divorcee is a subject of much discussion. However, they can all afford to wait until we know the answer to that initial question.

Now, according to the Bible, a marriage that has already been consummated cannot be annulled. The Bible contains a number of supplementary passages that seem to back it up just as strongly as any other passage that may back up a teaching of our holy religion. They all concur that it is forbidden for a man to separate what God has joined and apply this maxim to the relationship between a man and his wife. Jesus Christ reiterates the clear instruction multiple times.

The caution is a restriction against marrying one divorcee to another despite popular belief which is not the text's entire meaning. The practice of separating is specifically prohibited, and the illegality of remarrying is a natural outcome of this prohibition.

The popular belief that it is acceptable for married people to separate whenever they see it fit as long as they do not remarry is in direct opposition to what Jesus Christ said in His own words:

"So they are no longer two, but one flesh. What therefore God has joined together, let not man put asunder (separate)" (Matthew 19:6).

Although not widely observed, it appears that the prevailing opinion is that the separation, itself, is legal but that getting married again after a separation is prohibited. However, the act of separating is, itself, a clear violation of the commandment. Along with that, it involves all the negative aspects of allowing a second marriage except for one.

A man or a woman who divorces their spouse and does not remarry does not commit adultery; that is, they do not commit a second sin on top of the first. That is the only distinction between a separation and what is referred to as a divorce from the marriage bond.

Every separation of marriage disregards Paul's reasoning on why men should marry women and have wives. (Corinthians 7:2). When a married couple starts living apart, the true bond of marriage is broken. The estranged couple can cut all relations as a result of this separation. Both might be cut off from the benefits of each other's way of life. The wife might not be in a position to help or counsel the husband fully. The husband may not be able to lead or protect the wife.

Marriage is essentially dissolved when a married couple chooses to live apart. Marriage is practically dissolved because the husband

and wife are not allowed to behave in the same ways that married couples do. The restriction has only one detrimental effect. Due to their separation, the husband and wife abandon all of their marriage responsibilities. The children forfeit all of the advantages to which they are entitled from one parent and the majority of those from the other. Both of the couple practically live celibate lives despite the fact that they are only officially married.

Such a situation involves serious evils that are undervalued in many nations and, more importantly, in many churches. The majority of people, including Christians, either willfully ignore God's prohibition against separating husbands and wives or unwilfully disobey it. Those do usually interpret the prohibition on separating marriage as essentially forbidding marriage to those who have been divorced. That is a wholly fictitious interpretation, legally disregard and deny the value of the Word of God. One of the subjects that cause people the most confusion is how the law and the gospel relate to each other.

Some people place the law of Moses about marriage before the gospel while others place the gospel before the law. Some take neither the law nor the gospel but, instead, change both. Others completely abolish the law by introducing the gospel.

If a husband and a wife live together according to God's plan, it is a clear demonstration of a beautiful ambiance that prevails between them and their home, their Eden! In our minds' eye, we see a fairy vision of adoring submission and condescending fellowship, pure excitement and unbounded favor, a humble commitment and a fatherly grin, a flawless serenity, and some limitless complacency that prevails in the home. Everyone in the family is kind and indulgent toward one another showing respect and honor to people inside and outside of their own homes. Their home resembles the Garden of Eden which was beautiful with its meadow and flowers.

I cannot begin to portray a picture of a husband and wife living with God who is always revealing Himself to them and their children in their home, expanding their knowledge while also causing His joy to overflow. Every family member spends their days and lives in the house enjoying unparalleled pleasures.

Alas! Alas! Alas! It is nothing more than a dream! The separation of a husband and a wife interrupts the dream. The deadly fruit that was hanging from the household tree of the knowledge of good and evil has been plucked and eaten. We cannot stop to recount the harrowing story of the horrific injustices and the many evils that the serpent's path brought upon our nature and slimed it over with wickedness in many marriages without crying. Thus, to limit the section that forbids a man from separating what God has joined to such a division that will let the separated persons remarry, as many countries' public opinion does, is to take an unjustified liberty with the Bible.

The Obligation To Stay Married

The obligation which suggests that we may solemnly own that every married couple is under a higher obligation to remain married still stands. Marriage is like being a soldier in a battle; both spouses must follow the orders of their commanding officer. Of course, marriage involves a commitment to never remarry while the other spouse is still alive, but it also has a lot more ramifications. There is an adage that says, "No one marries their enemy."

Every marriage begins as an admirable union. Many couples meet with an earnest purpose, all conscious that they will marry till the end. It is important to note that being hostile to your spouse is not admirable. Living in harmony with all men is the best course of action, but married couples must always make an extra effort to living in harmony with each other.

Many people walk into marriage hoping to find the rock of confidence of an Adam or an Eve who God had flawlessly created. Evidently, this is simpler because there is wisdom among many counselors. But the reality of marriage is completely different. It is obvious that you cannot approach infallibility by combining more than two fallible humans. The analogy of the Garden of Eden can serve as a helpful reminder that a man and a woman combined are equal to fallibility.

Human behavior is thought to be hard to decipher by nature. No matter how responsible, loving, virtuous, and gracious a husband and a wife may be, there will inevitably be arguments at varying moments during their marriage life. Marriage is, therefore, a continuous strive for love, peace, unity, etc.

Once, Paul exhorted the Romans to strive. Three verses after really encouraging them to strive, he prays for the God of peace to be with them all. Lest anyone should think of me to be a woman of strife, they must read the verse as depicted by Paul:

"I appeal to you [I entreat you], brethren, for the sake of our Lord Jesus Christ and by the love [given by] the Spirit, to unite with me in earnest wrestling in prayer to God in my behalf." (Romans 15:30).

That is a holy strive. And I desire every couple to strive in prayer, forming a circle around God's throne, appealing to God for lasting love, peace, and unity, and praying until they are truly enveloped in God's love.

God's grace and love make human beings better in all relationships. Many marriages have become spiritually separated because of the lack of God's love. Love-filled words have been replaced with rude ones, and a minor disagreement escalates and degenerates into a war that is far fiercer than the war between Russia and Ukraine.

Many married couples need genuine repentance to break their stubborn habit. They share a home with their spouses, but many of them are divorced or separated in their hearts. Many once-loving spouses have become murderers in their hearts. I am referring to murders which John interprets to mean all expressions of unreasonable anger. A hidden murder is perpetrated by a husband or a wife who wishes their spouse was dead or otherwise wounded usually as a result of irrational anger. A spouse with a bad nature sits by the fireplace in a great number of households and murders their spouse in their thoughts.

They have allowed a repulsive, evil concept to take up residence in their minds, and as a result, they use words to throw arrows at the same spouse they swore to love and adore inside the homes where no human is privy to their actions. Such spouses sleep in different bedrooms from each other and, as a result, think, act, and plan separately. Even when they share a home, a married couple's marriage is effectively dissolved when they plan, act, and even sleep separately. Only God's magnifying glass will be able to count the number of broken marriages and homes.

Through His forensic counting, the world may one day learn how many lives have been ruined by the callous adultery of husbands and wives who have shattered those they promised to cherish. Once someone breaks their marriage vows, they also break all other commitments.

Separation from marriage, which eventually leads to divorce, is always motivated by hatred.

"For the Lord, the God of Israel, says: I hate divorce and marital separation and him who covers his garment [his wife] with violence. Therefore keep a watch upon your spirit [that it may be controlled by My Spirit], that you deal not treacherously and faithlessly [with your marriage mate] (Malachi 2:16).

Paul says that no one has ever hated their own flesh.

"For no man ever hated his own flesh, but nourishes and carefully protects and cherishes it, as Christ does the church." (Ephesians 5:29);

Less so will God, who is Love Itself, do so; yes, God is Love. The bond between God and us and that of a husband and wife is eternal just like He is.

The loving God, compelled by love itself, frowns at separation and divorce. He threatens, He denounces. His justice and holiness lead Him to use rough words towards His erring creatures who abuse their fellows. God does more: in infinite love, He chastens as well as rebukes.

Instead of fatherly caresses, the Father God wisely takes down the rod and lays it on the backs of those whom He most truly loves.

"For whom the Lord loves He chastens, And scourges every son whom He receives." (Hebrews 12:6 NKJV).

Those nearest to His heart and most approved of His soul among the sons of Adam have nevertheless to feel that "Our God is a consuming fire."

"Marriage is, therefore, a continuous strive for love, peace, unity, etc."

God Punishes Sin

Placed in the crucible, they are thrust into the white heat of the furnace, and there they are called to suffer so that their dross may be removed. God is angry with anyone who treats their spouse or another human cruelly and abusively. He characterizes the behavior as wicked. *"God is angry with the wicked every day."*

When you say that God is angry with the wicked every day, some modern god-makers tell you that God is too loving to do that, and that He cannot possibly be angry. They have created a brand-new god that is different from the ancient God of Israel. They assert that God loves everyone, has atoned for everyone, and will ultimately deliver every one, even Satan.

A president, a priest, a police officer, or a soldier who encourages criminal behavior, does not punish criminal behavior or does not become incensed by wickedness must be immediately removed from office.

Apostle Retired Samuel Ansong stated it best when he said: *"I have not stumbled on in the Bible."*

The holy, loving, and true God declares in the Bible:

"If you walk contrary to Me, I will walk contrary to you." "To the froward, he will show himself froward." "...curse and doomed to disappointment and destruction".

For it is written in the Scriptures:

"Cursed (accursed, devoted to destruction, doomed to eternal punishment) be everyone who does not continue to abide (live and remain) by all the precepts and commands written in the Book of the Law and to practice them" (Galatians 3:10).

God is made known as a God who " but Who will by no means clear the guilty, visiting the iniquity of the fathers upon the children and the children's children, to the third and fourth generation" (Exodus 34:7).

Divorce Makes Women More Vulnerable

Every thinking mind must have been compelled by Paul's tremendous truth about remaining married. A marriage that God ordains will endure forever and prosper in every way. The real reason why God forbade a man from separating what He had joined was to stop married people from divorcing. It is only to stop them from getting remarried after a divorce.

Even though we have thoughts of our own and are so far from being unlike God because we are intellectual beings, His thoughts will always be stronger and more complete than ours. Despite the fact that we are free agents with the ability to choose our own paths, some of which we navigate with great knowledge, our ways are earthly and cannot match God's, who is far above us.

In the Sermon on the Mount, Jesus made certain statements on His ultimate purpose:

"It hath been said, Whosoever shall put away his wife, let him give her writing of divorcement; but I say unto you, that whosoever shall put away his wife, saving for the cause of fornication, causes her to commit

adultery, and whosoever shall marry her that is divorced committeth adultery." (Matthew 5:31-32 KJV).

How can a husband induce adultery in his divorced wife save by putting her in a tempting situation. What kind of temptation is that - to be married? Absolutely to commit adultery! What a horrible situation this is! May every couple contemplating divorce have a chilling sense of fear as they weigh their options.

The term "temptation" has two meanings: first, that of being tested or afflicted, and second, that of being convinced or seduced into committing a sin. God tested Abraham, or tempted him, in the early part of their friendship, as He does with all of His people. God had only one sinless son, but He never had a son without temptations. Within the holy cloister of God's children, you won't be able to find anyone whom God hasn't permitted to be tried in love at some moment or in some form.

All meanings of the word "tempt" - including the unfavorable and challenging ones - are applicable to the claim.

All of God's people have experienced the temptation to sin. Satan, instantly, seeks to destroy the work of the Holy Spirit soon as he perceives a child of God renewed in heart and free from sins. Satan seeks to make the believer unhappy and reduce their usefulness by luring them into immorality.

AN ANALOGY

Those who are familiar with Satan's methods have discovered that there is a method to his temptations and that he will most likely target someone, especially a child of God, during specific periods and seasons. He has studied human nature for so long that he knows more about a man than man knows about themselves.

According to a skilled writer, the devil of old is quite different from the devil of the twenty-first century. Despite being the same evil spirit, his method of attack differs. In our traditional depictions of that terrible spirit, the devil of the Garden of Eden is always a black and filthy monster.

He was a provocateur, an accuser, and a persecutor who, through Jezebel, threatened prophets and through Nebuchadnezzar, cast men into the fire. The devil of the twenty-first century is a well-mannered gentleman who prefers to seduce and entice rather than force. Satan may ultimately want to persuade Mrs. Doe to engage in fornication or adultery, but he would not make the suggestion to her. Satan can, instead, start by making a great husband, Mr. Doe, into an alcoholic. And over time, this causes him to become a violent enemy to his wife and children.

Mrs. Doe's husband physically assaults her leaving her with bruises and being trampled on despite having a kind, loving personality that should have been loved like a delicate flower. Despite the prolonged family intervention, Mr. Doe, who is under the control of Satan, continues to display characteristics that are very similar to him. Mrs. Doe keeps going through the pain until her heart breaks with sorrow. When all efforts to assist Mr. Doe are unsuccessful, he divorces Mrs. Doe.

First, Mr. Doe may have been Mrs. Doe's sole financial supporter. She might have raised her children as a stay-at-home mother for a considerable length of time. She is now, instantaneously, exposed to any man who is prepared to assist her in exchange for sex since Mr. Doe is no longer in the picture.

A wealthy person may resist the temptation even if offered millions of dollars or more. However, a person with a small wallet and no food on the table cannot afford to lose a shilling. Due to Mrs. Doe's situation, the perpetrator might decide to take advantage of her.

To add but one more, with the exception of a small minority, the majority of women, who experience abuse and later get divorced from the person they had hoped would have changed, experience some combination of shame and guilt. No matter how hard they try, they are unable to immediately forget the marriage they have just left behind. The abuse they endure, both physically and emotionally, may cause serious soul damage.

Divorce is a severe, a difficult, and a confusing situation into which spouses fall. The physician may be confused by the location of a physically fractured bone, but what do they do when the bones of the soul are damaged? Compound fractures in the physical bone require significant difficulties in reassembling the broken sections in the hopes that further bone will grow and the member will be preserved. But if a soul is broken, how extremely cautious must a soul physician be if there is such a thing?

More than anything else during this trying time, Mrs. Doe, whose husband, Mr. Doe, has divorced her, needs the love and support of her loved ones. She needs the ideal sympathizers who can relate to her.

Typically, Satan, during these times, places traps on a divorcee's path that are closely linked to secrecy.

"For in vain is the net spread in the sight of any bird! (Proverbs 1:17).

Satan can carefully cover up his trap by using Mr. X who presents himself as the perfect husband to Mrs. Doe. It appears as though

Satan has educated him specifically to be Mr. Doe's exact opposite. If Mr. Doe had never offered gifts, Mr. X would have given many gifts. He charms Mrs. Doe by singing "Love, Love" and decorating her with "Love". Because Mrs. Doe's heart is broken, it is very easy for her to mistakenly call anything that Mr. X does "Love." She, thus, falls for Mr. X and marries him, only to realize that he is just another, if not the worst, version of Mr. Doe. Both Mrs. Doe and Mr. X commit adultery to marry.

Yet, Mr. Doe is the ultimate culprit, for he set Mrs. Doe up for the sin of adultery. In Mrs. Doe's instance, true marriage is one type of adultery, but it's not the only kind. If Mrs. Doe is unable to marry, the desire to commit adultery in those other forms will increase for her, who is estranged from Mr. Doe.

Mr. Doe, who has divorced Mrs. Doe, makes Mrs. Doe know this temptation. She basically lives in an unmarried condition, making her vulnerable to temptations for fleshly sins like adultery. Mrs. Doe cannot marry her way out of those temptations like other women may. She is particularly susceptible to those temptations because of the judgment of Jesus Christ.

Mrs. Doe cannot get married, but she can have adultery. She faces such powerful temptations that Jesus says anyone who exposes her to them will be condemned to "cause her to commit adultery".

When Christians believe they are in double danger in such a situation as Mrs. Doe, it happens regularly that they are forced to be more vigilant. The threat might then be avoided by their readiness to handle it. Prevention is preferable to cure. It is preferable to be so well-prepared that the devil won't attack you rather than to put up with the dangers of the battle even if you win.

Christians Are Not Encouraged To Divorce

Paul warns us by sharing a Divine FACT:

"You were bought with a price [purchased with a preciousness and paid for, made His own]. So then, honor God and bring glory to Him in your body." 1 Corinthians 6:20

"You did not make yourselves" or "You do not preserve themselves: it is God who keeps you alive; you would die if He withheld His breath."

The reasons for obeying the great Lawgiver of marriage may come from creation. And several reasons for sanctity may be supported by the preservation of Divine Providence. Surely, we should be obedient to the One who provides for, sustains, and feeds our life. Here, divorce is explicitly forbidden without any mention of being married again. The justification presented for it appears to be the same as what Jesus Christ stated in the Sermon on the Mount. In order to avoid separating it from its context, let's briefly review Paul's earlier claims that nothing can be lost by neglect.

Now, Paul says: *"You are bought with a price."* Thus, the conclusion drawn from it is, "I have no right to do whatever I want by myself." As a Christian, I have no power to do anything to another human body that would pollute it because it is not my own. The apostle is primarily addressing the sins of the flesh when he says:

"Food [is intended] for the stomach and the stomach for food, but God will finally end [the functions of] both and bring them to nothing. The body is not intended for sexual immorality, but [is intended] for the Lord, and the Lord [is intended] for the body [to save, sanctify, and raise it again]." (1 Corinthians 6:13).

Because our bodies are not our own but rather, the members of Jesus Christ, we have no right to practice sexual immorality. He would say the same about alcoholism, gluttony, abusiveness, and even about an inordinate desire for money that harms one's health when not handled with care.

Every part of our body belongs to God; it is His property; He has purchased it, and we have no right to desecrate or harm that which is dedicated to Him "with a price." Any moral person would be more concerned if something were to happen to someone else's property while it was in his or her care than if it were their own. The wife is, therefore, not her own. She gave herself away on a great and memorable wedding day. And she wears the golden ring on her finger as a reminder of that day.

When she gave herself over to her husband, she did not cry, and the well-wishers did not sing along with the wedding bell "Abuse March". She remembers her wedding day with radiant excitement; it was a happy day for her. Even though she no longer belongs to anyone, she has no regrets about giving herself away and would do it all over again for the same devoted owner. She should find comfort in her husband's home, and the husband should know that he is not his own; he does not desire that he is. The fact that she is her husband does not imply her enslavement but rather, her happiness. He has dedicated himself, body, soul, and spirit, to the wonderful Bridegroom of his heart; he is also wedded to Jesus Christ. He became a Christian on the wedding day of his genuine life, and he should look back on it with delight and wonder.

In the same chapter is this passage:

"But if she does [separate from and divorce him], let her remain single or else be reconciled to her husband. And [I charge] the husband [also] that he should not put away or divorce his wife." (1 Corinthians 7:11).

Paul says: "I command, yet not I but the Lord:" It seems to imply that the commentary he is about to take on some of the Lord's remarks is inspired. The words discussed appear to be some of those mentioned in the Gospel of Mark.

"What therefore God has united (joined together), let not man separate or divide" (Mark 10:9).

Yet again:

"But I tell you, Whoever dismisses and repudiates and divorces his wife, except on the grounds of unfaithfulness (sexual immorality), causes her to commit adultery, and whoever marries a woman who has been divorced commits adultery" (Matthew 5:32).

Jesus Christ now exposes the truth that separating a man and his wife does not relieve them of the charge of adultery should they remarry, despite the fact that the prohibition to separate what God had joined had previously been given. Paul presents this idea as a rule. He begins by stating two rules that when combined, reiterate a commandment made by Jesus:

"Let not the woman depart from her husband." "Let not the man put away his wife."

The third precept he adds incorporates the teachings of Jesus Christ:

"Now as to the matters of which you wrote me. It is well [and by that I mean advantageious, expedient, profitable, and wholesome] for a man not to touch a woman [to cohabit with her] but to remain unmarried." (1 Corinthians 7:1).

In essence, this is similar to the scriptures cited below that whenever a woman is divorced, and she gets married to another man, she commits adultery:

"But to the married people I give charge – not I but the Lord – that the wife is not to separate from her husband. But if she does [separate from and divorce him], let her remain single or else be reconciled to her husband. And [I charge] the husband [also] that he should not put away or divorce his wife." (1 Corinthians 7:10-11)

Paul's structure clarifies Jesus Christ's teachings by presenting them from a different angle and considering them all as laws. Thus, it would seem that the words of Jesus Christ involve two independent and distinct teachings.

A woman must be faithful to her husband; nevertheless, if she were to act in such a misguided manner, she would be in violation of another principle that forbids marriage. A different and separate law forbids marriage. She is instructed to make amends if she has broken her marriage vows which she is prohibited from doing. She is still to remain single if she chooses to disregard both of those rules. Thus, Paul adds:

"To the rest I declare - I, not the Lord [for Jesus did not discuss this] - that if any brother has a wife who does not believe [in Christ] and she consents to live with him, he should not leave or divorce her" (1 Corinthians 7:12).

Paul explains here: *"To the rest speak I, not the Lord."* It is not to be supposed that by this, he meant to admit that he was not writing by inspiration. Earlier, he had stated: *"I command, yet not I but the Lord."*

The two sentences should be interpreted collectively. In the beginning, Paul was reiterating a teaching that had come directly from the mouth of Jesus Christ; nevertheless, what he is about to say is simply an application of Jesus's theology to a specific situation - that of a Christian who is unequally yoked with an atheist. (1 Corinthians 7:12-15).

Paul decides that the statute that prohibits separation still applies in this situation. Both the Christian man and the Christian lady are not to put away their worldly spouses. The God they did not know at the time of their marriage union does not break their bond even if one of them has come to know Him. Even though they were godless, they were together. They are not to be separated because one of them converted to Christianity. The only thing Paul permits is that the Christian may agree without sinning if the unbelievers insist on a separation; he or she is not in slavery. Christian Law is quite stringent in that it prevents divorce between husband and wife. It does not support the widely held belief that married people can agree to divorce if they do not remarry.

A Certificate Of Divorce

"And when she departs out of his house she goes and marries another man," (Deuteronomy 24:2).

Examining the Mosaic Law makes it very evident that the Divine Lawgiver favored a complete severance of the marriage connection allowing the parties to marry to the partial divorce that was left. While all of its constructive obligations were removed or ignored, it was only a negative constraint. This is the commandment that Moses gave, which Jesus Christ mentioned repeatedly.

"When a man takes a wife and marries her, if then she finds no favor in his eyes because he has found some indecency in her, and he writes her a bill of divorce, puts it in her hand, and sends her out of his house,

And when she departs out of his house she goes and marries another man, And if the latter husband dislikes her and writes her a bill of divorce and puts it in her hand and sends her out of his house, or if the latter husband dies, who took her as his wife, Then her former husband, who sent her away, may not take her again to be his wife after she is defiled. For that is an abomination before the Lord; and you shall not bring guilt upon the land which the Lord your God gives you as an inheritance." (Deuteronomy 24:1-4).

Any separation is prohibited here, excluding those that concern the ability to get married. If a man has a wife who he despises and wants to divorce, he must follow a specific path that is twice and in great length described throughout the span of the four verses. If he does so with a divorce decree in hand, she is free to leave his home and marry someone else. He is not permitted to send her away without a divorce decree. In actuality, the certificate of divorce was always prepared in a specific format that gave the divorced woman express permission to get married. The Hebrew word for the divorce decree is *get*. The Mishna claims that the following words make up its core component. If the husband said:

"*Thou art herewith permitted to be married to any man, except to my father or to your father, to my brother or to your brother, to a slave or to a non-Israelite," or to any other person with whom she is interdicted by law to marry, the Get is valid.*"

"According to the Rabbi Jehudah, this is the crucial component: "Thou hast here from me a writing of separation and a document of dismissal, that thou may go and be married to any man thou mayest like."

Whatever the writing's format, it was clear from the law that a divorced woman might marry. The husband might send his wife outside of his home once he has handed it to her.

"And when she departs out of his house she goes and marries another man." (Deuteronomy 24:2).

The Basis For A Permited Divorce In The Bible

Moses apparently gave the children of Israel this law as a result of their hard hearts, Deuteronomy 24:1-4. Some scholars have theorized that Jesus Christ was trying to convey the idea that men's hearts were so hard that they would kill or mistreat spouses who had failed to win their favor.

Giving the woman the ability to divorce her husband would have been a more evident form of protection if the husband's brutality during the marriage had been evil to be feared. It appears more likely that the issue the rule intended to address was sending a woman out into the world where she would be vulnerable to all the temptations and challenges of single life without having the ability to ask a spouse for help.

The Divine Lawgiver predicted that because of the hardness of their hearts, they would force their spouses outside. Although it was not always the case, Moses desired that women in that situation have the ability to get married. This was a divergence from the Divine law of marriage which He alone could approve and did approve because men, in their heartlessness, would not abide by the basic commandment. This is demonstrated by the care that was taken to grant the divorced woman the right to marry.

Permimission To Divorce Is Not An Exiate To Sin

Jesus Christ does not authorize the harshness that the Mosaic Law prohibited. He remembers marriage as a simple institution where there is no room for any kind of separation. He reiterates the directive that a man should remain faithful to his wife, affirms the idea that they are one flesh, and introduces the principle that men should not separate them in light of this idea. Thus, Jesus Christ completely opposes any kind of separation. He further declares that if anyone, disregarding his prohibition, shall put away his wife and marry another, he will be guilty of adultery.

He does not mention the archaic institution or give the admonition that He has already declared to follow it in the Sermon on the Mount. There, He says:

"I say to you: whoever dismisses (repudiates, divorces) his wife, except for unchastity, and marries another commits adultery, and he who marries a divorced woman commits adultery." (Matthew 19:9).

Moses prohibited every separation without a bill of divorce or any separation without the right to marry. The divorce decree served as authorization to marry another man. Jesus Christ condemns all putting away, whether or not there is a divorce decree or permission to marry someone else. He declares that anyone who puts his wife away, even in the manner instructed by Moses, causes her to commit adultery; and that anyone who marries her also commits adultery, repealing the forgiveness given by Moses of putting a woman away if she were permitted to marry again. He encourages her to commit adultery by putting her in a position where doing so would be highly tempting. This concludes the Sermon on the

Mount's explanation of this aspect of the topic. Jesus Christ repeals the law that permits a bill of divorce subject to that saving, but He does not repeal the law that banned men from divorcing their wives without one. This was a fundamental tenet of the marriage concept, and it is repeated in words: *"Whosoever puts away his wife causes her to commit adultery."* She should not get a divorce because of the temptation to commit adultery that she will face. If she is not allowed to marry, those temptations will increase rather than decrease. (Matthew 5:31-32).

THE LAW OF MARRIAGE AND TYPES OF MARRIAGE SEPARATION

Marriage is the cornerstone of any civilization. Therefore, anyone marrying must consider the immediate welfare of the community. It is, therefore, impossible to deny the United States of America the ability to pass legislation on it. Like all others, they should accurately explain the law of God. No earthly authority can make the State right if she misinterprets the law or even passes a law without taking the Divine rule into account. Fortunately, the State gives everyone the freedom to choose not to get married or to marry whomever they want with very few exceptions. She sees some of the Christian restrictions to marriage between specific people in this.

Many countries, like the USA, do not require a priest to officiate each particular marriage. Hence, if marriage laws are faulty, they are nonetheless inherently liberal and cannot violate anyone's conscience.

The State did not enact any laws regarding matrimonial issues during the Middle Ages, and her courts did not hear any cases. The

Church created and implemented the law and was given control of the entire situation. The State only recognized her judgments as being final.

The Church has a right to explain the marriage law for her own ends. This had nothing to do with the State and involved no ally right to overrule the State's decisions or otherwise interfere with temporal rights. However, the State recognized the Church's civil matters judgments. The State always had the right to revoke the authority that she had granted to the Church in this fashion, but not the initial authority that the Church had to enact laws regarding marriage from a spiritual perspective. Contracting an illegal marriage, remaining in it after it has been consummated, or cohabiting apart from a lawful spouse are all crimes that, like all sins, weaken the spiritual condition of the person who does them. The Church has jurisdiction over all sins.

Marriage-related disputes were seen as falling under the purview of canon law and ecclesiastical courts during the Middle Ages. According to English usage, there were three categories of them: divorce proceedings, restitution of conjugal rights, and judicial dissolution of marriage.

Two types of processes, each with a very distinct character and neither of which were legitimate divorce proceedings, were included in the first class. A legitimate marriage is dissolved through a divorce. However, it is a fundamental tenet of canon law that a legitimate marriage cannot be annulled.

Mensa Et Thoro

However, that law recognizes two situations that it refers to as divorce: the first is a statement that a purported marriage is null and void. Although the formalities of a marriage may have been followed, the parties involved were not legally married. The ecclesiastical courts had the authority to declare such unions null and void. A vinculo matrimonii is the legal term for such a declaration.

The alternative option, referred to as a divorce, allowed or ordered married people to live apart from each other while the marriage remained intact.

A mensa et thoro divorce was used to describe this. There were four different types of matrimonial reasons back then: vinculo matrimonii divorces, mensa et thoro divorces, restitution of conjugal rights, and judicial dissolution of marriage.

Bypassing the first of those processes for the time being, the second and third can be taken into consideration jointly. They are correlated with one another. Both ask the same question but do it in different ways and in distinct contexts. In one, the person who wants to live apart from their spouse seeks permission to do so implying protection. In the second, the person who wants to leave has abandoned their friend without permission, and the deserted person is trying to compel them to return. Both of those cases were undoubtedly requests for advice and help from the diocese's bishop at their outset. The broad notion that married people must live together as husband and wife is stated in plain terms by the apostle, Paul.

However, specific situations could occur that make carrying out that responsibility challenging. One of the marriage's parties may not be able to cohabitate with the other due to the challenges. The priest was the best person to settle such issues since he was familiar with Divine law, stood impartially between the parties, and had power over both. Whether the unusual circumstances of the case were such to make it an exception to the general norm was the issue that he had to resolve. People who were unsure of the path they were required to take at a conscientious age naturally turned to their priest for guidance. Usually, his decision would end the dispute; however, if it did not, the ancient discipline allowed him the authority to enforce it by excommunication.

Excommunication, however, was merely a conscience-based request. When the priest's decision prompts the offender's conscience and, if necessary, by excommunication, it may work in such a way as to result in a complete reconciliation. When religious trials took on a forensic character, the priest's advice turned into a direct exercise of his authority. One of two forms was used. A divorce, known as a mensa et thoro was requested when the parties were still cohabitating. It was possible for the individual who had moved out to submit a similar application to formally end their relationship if one had separated from the other. This became the standard course of action; the unhappy party left and requested a legal separation, or as it was later known, a divorce, or mensa et thoro.

However, if a person did not want to be legally separated, they might seek a decision to restore conjugal rights which would order the person who had left to return. Over time, the priest ceased to personally judge religious cases. They were tried by judges who, whether or not they were members of the clergy, were essentially attorneys who made decisions based on rules and precedents and with a lawyerly attitude.

Another shift has now occurred, and marriage cases are now decided by a simple lay judge appointed by the State. The court processes for the restoration of conjugal rights can only be a fantasy under such circumstances. In the old system, a reunion of feelings might have resulted from the return of the departing person, which was either directly or indirectly the result of conscience. The religious court could issue its decree in light of what came next, but it was unlikely to have many positive consequences. If applied to a recusant wife, it would give her husband custody of her person. Previously, the husband had the power to ensure outward loyalty thanks to the law of the land and social conventions. However, it is improbable that a judge might order the restoration of emotions, the most important conjugal rights.

The law today has undergone significant changes as have society's practices. If a recusant woman was treated harshly, the same court that gave her husband custody again would issue her a judicial separation for cruelty. It is difficult to see how a ruling requiring a husband to return to his abandoned wife could have any positive results.

Therefore, a formal decision is rarely sought in cases of divorce (a mensa et thoro) which the recent act of Parliament refers to by its proper term, judicial separation, until after a separation by agreement or in another manner has occurred. Then, it is sought purely for civil reasons. It will give the separate legal status, serve as a response to any request for the restoration of conjugal rights, free the wife from the burden of legal responsibility that still rests with the husband, and serve as the basis for a request for alimony, or a provision for her support at her husband's expense.

However, because a judicial separation has been rejected, husbands and wives do not currently cohabitate. The State may provide for judicial separations for the relevant purposes. Regardless of rules imposed by humans on the matter, a Christian's conscience will continue to be seriously troubled. A person who considers requesting a judicial separation, or, as it is still known in many nations, a divorce, or mensa et thoro, must first determine if doing so they would not violate divine law given the circumstances.

Vinculo Matrimonii

A divorce, also known as a vinculo matrimonii, is a legal procedure to declare a marriage legally null. This procedure has a varied history. The process, initiated by the authority of the Church, was originally known as pro salute animnarum, or for the health of the affected people's souls.

It was meant to put an end to their current lifestyle of wickedness. The solution was left to the sinners' consciences as the Church's discipline deteriorated.

In the interim, the Latin Church had increased the intermarriage bans to the point where it was challenging for anyone of any status to find someone nearby who was of equal rank with whom he or she might legitimately marry.

The Popes, who had the authority to give dispensations and sell them for a high price, may have been motivated to multiply the bans to increase their financial gain. They achieved that goal but turned out to be a major moral evil. The fact that they could be bought with money kept the restrictions from ingraining themselves in people's consciousness. They were expensive; therefore, marriages, for which they were required, were often solemnized without them, sometimes without the parties' knowledge that their relationships fell within the prohibited degrees.

A dispensation could also have a formal flaw, and formal requirements were strictly upheld when it was profitable. There were no longer any such exemptions. It was simple to assert - often with accuracy - that a dispensation had been obtained through fraud or deceit if it had no formal flaws. Overall, the system gave powerful men the ability to arbitrarily divorce their wives because of how easy it was for them to do so. In theory, the same facility was available to the women, but not in reality.

THE CHURCH HAD A SUPERIOR JURIDICTION ON MARRIAGE

A new set of guiding concepts guided the marital judication process. Its purpose was to prevent people from falsely claiming or jactitation that they were married to specific people. It is unlikely that such a practice has ever been so pervasive or malicious as to call for a fix. However, one was offered.

Unless a person built up a defense that the brag was properly grounded, it seems that all that was required to secure a ruling prohibiting the person complained about from repeating the boast was to demonstrate that he or she had said it. The question of whether a marriage between the parties had actually been solemnized would then need to be answered, followed by a question about the legality of that marriage. These two probes both fell under the purview of the Church. The whole jurisdiction in matrimonial matters had been given to the Church by the State which had adopted the ecclesiastical law of marriage.

It is still the case in England - at least there hasn't been a formal legislative change - that the civil court must submit any problem that involves just the topic of marriage and no other issue to the priest of the diocese. Those situations now hardly ever happen. When the question of whether someone is married or not is entangled with another subject, as it usually is, the jury trial process must be followed. It was only logical to give the religious court jurisdiction when trying to right an injustice like the legalization of marriage.

The process is uncommon; however, there was a noteworthy example in the previous century. It was a clever attempt to utilize it to free married people from engagements that they were tired of. A lawsuit for the judication of marriage was filed against the actual husband. The marriage had never been acknowledged in public and had been kept private. Complicity resulted in the suppression of the evidence, and the husband was forbidden from claiming the marriage. The woman believed she was still legally single and went as Mrs. Brown or Miss Livingston, the name she had previously used before becoming Duchess of York.

Following the bigamy trial, it was determined that the Church Court's punishment had no impact on her State of affairs. The court action has since been used to demonstrate that two young people were not made man and wife as a result of the marriage ceremony being used in the sport.

Over time, the State's policies underwent a transformation. Instead of ceding any of her sovereignty to the Church, she encroached on it and eventually started dictating church law.

In England, the marriage eventually came to be seen as solely falling under state control. However, marriage cases continued to be heard in courts that were ostensibly religious but had completely lost all traces of their religious nature due to secularization. A court that was ostensibly civil took over the courts' marriage authority years later.

The Compromise

In the traditional sense of the word, there have never been any religious courts in America, Ghana or anywhere. Prior to the Revolution, there were no courts to administer the marriage laws which were the same throughout the colonies and the mother nation. They had little opportunities in a dispersed population with generally good morality. There were no provisions made during the Revolution for the administration of justice in marriage cases. But over time, queries regarding divorce surfaced.

State legislatures increasingly gained the power to allow married spouses to live apart from one another and even to dissolve the marriage with the commendable exception of a few places. They disregarded divine law and used those presumed powers according to their own judgment of expediency. Even more so, they came to corruptly use them.

Members would trade votes in exchange for favors, help advance desired initiatives, or even just the expectation that the favor would be returned in some fashion. Divorces could be obtained for any cause and without considering the alleged facts. Every day, more and more leniencies were added to the entire marriage statute. Conjugal rights have never been restored, and marriage has never been formally recognized. Such incidents were previously unheard of in America, in Ghana and in other counties. Laws prohibiting the marriage of children and marriages within the ranges prohibited by Leviticus were passed soon after the Revolution.

Although there may not be a state where the more egregious forms of incestuous mixing are not prohibited and penalized in civil courts, most of the states have changed their laws to allow for a number of incestuous marriages.

There has been a general loosening of view on topics related to marriage as a result of those repeals and the legislative divorces. A few people are partially protected from this due to religious principles, and a few more are by some level of worldly sophistication. Even the legislators, who had hijacked and misused their authority over divorce, have become concerned about the current condition of affairs.

Instead, they have given the civil courts the authority to award legal divorces, including mensa et thoro and vinculo matrimonii under situations that are specified by law. The laws are frequently in conflict with the law of God since they are based on faulty principles. Every action helps to support the delusion that marriage cases are the only province of the State, which is untrue.

That she is an infallible interpreter of the correct application of the Divine laws of marriage has apparently been hastily inferred from this. This is untrue, and she doesn't even make an effort to interpret it. She enacts laws based on her clumsy and frequently personal ideas of practicality. Christians must, therefore, utilize their own private conscience on this topic, and that conscience must have a standard by which to evaluate issues that may be brought up.

The Revealed Law's rule is generally straightforward although men have raised many doubts about its intent. Church officials and private individuals are left to decide those issues on their own.

Some church officials have accomplished little. The laws of many Churches are her own, and they seem to be far stricter and more onerous than the Divine law. Although, perhaps, more so than those of any other denomination, her regulations between her professed system of dispensations and her unavowed system of connivance are not particularly rigorous. There has not been much action from the Protestant Episcopal Church. Even if the Presbyterian Communion has made more progress than any other group of Protestants, even her steps have been hesitant and unsure. Almost nothing has been done by the other denominations. People have embraced the law of the land and the conventional law of public opinion as their norms of action because they lack the moral courage to uphold the Divine law and interpret it for themselves.

Divine Guideline

When people conform to the law of a land and conventional law of public opinion, they tend to believe that they are blameless. Sometimes, they do not feel obligated to follow the law of the land. If people believe they may avoid shameful punishment and that the accepted morality of society will absolve their behavior, they often choose to disobey it. However, neither of those codes suffices as a reference.

Practically speaking, neither of them makes any mention of the relationship between man and God or the Revealed Law which man is required to obey.

Men's morals have consequently deteriorated to an extremely low level, particularly in regard to marital-related issues. All Christians recognize the necessity of the guidelines found in the Divine Word about these matters. Those guidelines make up the Christian view on marriage. Unfortunately, only a small percentage of them are upheld by either national law or popular opinion; both oppose some of them. As a result, there has been a significant loosening of the rules which can only be fixed by changing how the general public feels about things. The sole tool available for this task is the individual conscience.

Although there is little chance that it can be done, it should be tried. Perhaps, the only thing Christians can do is maintain a conscience that has not been hurt by Divine intervention in every situation. By enlightening the individual conscience which needs to be reminded of the laws that are written out in the Holy Scriptures, this book seeks to aid people in doing so.

CHAPTER 07

COMPASSION FOR THE IGNORANT

People become incredibly foolish when they do not learn from God. Satan ruthlessly gives people the opportunity to demonstrate their ignorance if they reject the counsel that comes from above. When a husband and a wife do not collectively prostrate themselves before God and His terms, they quickly create an idol out of themselves.

By submitting to their own terms in marriage, the husband and the wife create an image of themselves and degrade themselves. That is what happens when a couple rejects the biblical evidence of God's laws for marriage right from the beginning.

From a great number of such husbands and wives, the world's system has evolved terms that are a thousand times more ludicrous than any attempt to interpreting the Bible's terms of marriage. And God has left them to grope for another if they will not accept His solution to the problem.

Everyone, save them, can see right through and laugh at the terms the world uses to solve marital issues because they are so absurd.

When we depart from God and His terms, humanity is nothing and has nowhere to go. And in those instances when there are issues in marriage, what greater counseling can an ignorant person or world offer to the husband and wife for them to finish the marriage race?

What scripture or example can the world, which is ignorant of the actuality of real marriage, commend the Christian for? One of the largest beliefs in the world which has prided itself on being freethinking since its inception is now discovered stumbling into its grave and holding fast to the utter nonsense that since God only created one sex, men and women can marry one another. They have carved out broken, empty wells for themselves because they do not care to have God in their hearts and have abandoned the solid foundation of marriage institutions.

An article that was updated on February 26, 2023, reported that 7.2 percent of Americans were identified as lesbian, gay, bisexual, transgender, or other than straight or heterosexual. Since Gallup began tracking LGBT identity in 2012, the rate has doubled.

In 2023, over 210 million voters will be registered in the US. Various political parties, including Democrats, Republicans, Independents, and Libertarians, are represented among those voters. Approximately 38.8 million people are Republican Party registered voters. Around 49 million people are said to be Democratic voters.

We thank God that we do not decide to vote on the sexes of human beings in this manner. We do not subject our Christian beliefs to any such judiciary because we do not have such complete faith in the infallibility of majorities. However, if we had chosen to put gender identity or sex identification up for a vote between the two major parties in America, our ideas might have earned a smaller majority or greater majority depending on which party is voted for or against.

The "Yes" side may have won if a vote on the doctrine of Christian gender identity had been held in 2023. According to a Statista Research Department survey dated January 9, 2023, around five out of ten respondents support companies and brands that actively advocate equality for LGBT individuals. In a global poll done in 2021, 47% of participants said as much. In addition, 55% of those surveyed agreed that rules prohibiting discrimination against LGBT individuals in work, education, housing, social services, and other areas should be passed. I am not sure how many people would vote in favor of it or against it if the truth of gender identity were put to the vote right now throughout the entire world.

Furthermore, even if all voters were Christians and only those who sincerely believed in Jesus Christ were allowed to vote, regardless of how they felt about issues such as the ideal of marriage or gender identity, Christians would still lose because there are 2.6 billion Christians in the world, out of an estimated 8 billion people.

I sincerely hope that no one is so naive as to believe that just because we are the minority, we must inevitably be wrong regarding gender identity and how marriage should be handled. Let Christians remember that, if not now, then at some point in the past, every great truth was believed by a very small minority. Every great truth - whether it be found in the world of science, theology, or politics - is initially, and for a very long time, cherished by small minorities, and in all of proverbial literature, there is no saying more destructive than that "Everyone must be telling the truth."

Let's say Millicent has believed that the moon is an oblate spheroid, or a ball with a slightly flattened shape, all of her life. Her perception of the moon's shape abruptly shifts, and she now thinks it is shaped like a triangle. Then Millicent visits Davis' astronaut friend who has been trained to fly in space, run a spacecraft, or perform jobs related to human space exploration. After that, Millicent tells Davis:

"I no longer believe the Moon is an oblate spheroid, but I know it has a triangle form."

Davis could only smile at Millicent and say:

"Your viewpoint is meaningless because it doesn't change the truth. If you believe that the moon has suddenly changed into a triangle, the best way to disprove me is not to debate what shape you believe the moon should be but rather go visit my Hubble Telescope and observe the moon's shape."

The truth about gender identity follows the same pattern. The popular saying goes: "Man is to marry a man, and woman a woman." That does not disprove it. Is that stated in the Bible? That is the question. Can we read about a marriage between a man and a man or a woman and a woman? This is the other side of the question. Or do we only read about the first and subsequent marriages of a man and a woman?

Whether the world agrees with it or not, the only marriage described in the Bible is that of a man and a woman. Christians only need to report the information they find there. No one can transform the theories of gender identity into a form that the world would like, just as Davis was unable to alter the moon's shape in order to appease Millicent. The only thing that Davis, the astronaut, does is show a picture of the moon and state: *"That is how the shape of the moon is in the sky"*. Then, in order to confirm that it is true, Millicent must look up at the sky.

As Christians, all we need to do is share with the world what we learn from the Bible. It does not mean it is wrong if they don't like it, and we shouldn't worry about it either. The only thing is, Is it in the Bible? If it is there, we shall not stop to prove it.

Ignorance of any kind, like darkness, is bad; knowledge, on the other hand, is light, depending on the kind, excellent, better, or best. The ignorance of the world toward God, the ideal marriage, gender identity, love, and forgiveness are something for which they should be held accountable, but they should also be pitied.

Let every Christian's heart reach forth in love wherever we see ignorance regarding the things of God. However, let us pray to God with love and approach our endeavors with sincere compassion so that people's ignorance may be eradicated. It will be true of us as well if we are children of God, just like our great High Priest, then we will "have compassion on the ignorant".

"He is able to exercise gentleness and forbearance toward the ignorant and erring, since he himself also is liable to moral weakness and physical infirmity" (Hebrews 5:2).

*"Whether the world agrees with it or not,
the only marriage described in the Bible
is that of a man and a woman."*

IGNORANCE OF DIVORCE

The word "ignorance" could be translated as "inadvertence". Inadvertent ignorance is a form of acted ignorance: many husbands and wives have made mistakes in seeking divorce due to lack of thought, failing to take into account the consequences of their actions, the direction they are taking, or even what thinking initially advises.

Such couples, themselves, make mistakes because they did not study to be correct. They acted recklessly and quickly when taking the first course that presented itself. This form of sin is often committed, especially in divorce disputes. Even though there is no malicious intent, wrong is, nevertheless, committed. Some husbands and wives believed it was preferable to let their spouses leave if they could find a better one since they felt they were harming them by not being the ideal spouse.

One negligent act can result in a thousand mistakes. Both a lack of heart and a lack of thought can result in evil. Therefore, inadvertent sins are surely common among married couples, and in this uncertain, careless, reckless world, they are probably going to get worse.

Many husbands and wives do not give their acts enough thought; they do not pay enough attention to their steps. Life, especially marriage, should be a meticulous work of art, with every line and shade the result of research and consideration. Whatever kind of life a Christian leads on this earth, it is for eternity. But tragically, many individuals tend to judge life only based on their current perception. As a result, many people seem more motivated to accomplish a lot more than a lot well.

What Have I (Divorcee) Done

What should a husband and a wife do if they realize that their divorce was caused by ignorance and mistake? Do they truly suffer any guilt? Every decision a Christian makes reflects Jesus' viewpoint and judgment, not the church or another deity's, but God's Himself.

Every individual has been endowed by God with a head on their shoulders, including husbands and wives. Everyone must think with their own head, not that of their spouse, parent, or friend. God endowed our parents, friends, and children with judgment. God makes His own judgment. He established His own judgment which is excellent. Husbands and wives have been gifted with the ability to judge, and they should each judge on their own.

"If anyone sins and does any of the things the Lord has forbidden, though he was not aware of it, yet he is guilty and shall bear his iniquity." (Leviticus 5:17).

Because an ignorant divorced husband and wife are implicated in the guilt of sin, sins of ignorance are actually sins that require repentance. However, it is evident that the degree of guilt for ignorance versus knowing and willful actions differs substantially.

"And that servant who knew his master's will but did not get ready or act as he would wish him to act shall be beaten with many [lashes]." (Luke 12:47).

The husband and wife who were ignorant of God's admonition against divorce might face less punishment than the willful offender, but they still risk being beaten and given a beating with stripes, some of which will be far more than the couple may be willing to accept. The least scratches from the hand of justice will be sufficient to severely harm them.

Decent people have been reduced to groaning in anguish and lying in the dust as a result of the punishment of divorce. God, nonetheless, punishes ignorance-based sins.

"Therefore My people go into captivity [to their enemies] without knowing it and because they have no knowledge [of God]. And their honorable men [their glory] are famished, and their common people are parched with thirst". (Isaiah 5:13).

Hosea made that very clear when he said:

"My people are destroyed for lack of knowledge; because you [the priestly nation] have rejected knowledge, I will also reject you that you shall be no priest to Me; seeing you have forgotten the law of your God, I will also forget your children." (Hosea 4:6).

"Husbands and wives have been gifted with the ability to judge, and they should each judge on their own."

Living As A Divorcee

The Levitical law not only considered the likelihood that people would ignorantly break the law, but it also included provisions for it. The law, therefore, included specific provisions for ignorance-related sins, and one of them began with these words:

"If a person sins, and commits any of these things which are forbidden to be done by the commandments of the Lord, though he does not know it, yet he is guilty and shall bear his iniquity" (Leviticus 5:17).

We need not travel far, for we are sure that ignorance-related sins are possible based on our personal observations and experience. Many husbands and wives have committed that kind of sin, and when they were convinced of it, they were forced to mourn it bitterly. Even though some spouses earlier thought it was acceptable, there are many abuses, separations, and divorces that they have previously allowed themselves to be a part of and would never do so again because they understand how awful it is. Such spouses experience sorrow over their ignorance-based sins which their uninformed consciences would never experience if they were not genuinely ignorant.

Divorce is one of the life tragedies that Satan manages to use to shame the culprit and the victim. It is like a sin of commission that is an in-equity of excess and an omission an in-equity of falling short. Divorce is like a sin against God and man, especially against the innocent children in the family who never asked to be given to by a husband and a wife who decide not to continue their marriage race.

Even after many years, divorce may continuously aggravate its victims when they want to transition into another life. When those people who have suffered such terrible experiences from abuse through to divorce share their experience, they never end without saying: "It is a very terrible experience."

I don't intend to go through the extensive list of experiences; rather, I want to give divorcees, especially the innocent ones who unfortunately found themselves in an unsuitable relationship, hope in Jesus Christ; and also, admonish those of us who associate with the "Divorcee" to act appropriately around them because they are not less human because they are divorcees.

> *"Divorce is one of the life tragedies that Satan manages to use to shame the culprit and the victim."*

Not A Capital Punishment

God is a compassionate parent because He provided a sacrifice to atone for the guilt of ignorance-based sins preventing the guilty from losing hope.

"If any one of the common people sins unwittingly in doing anything the Lord has commanded not to be done, and is guilty, When the sin which he has committed is made known to him, he shall bring for his offering a goat, a female without blemish, for his sin which he has committed" (Leviticus 4:27-28).

So, after realizing their mistake, a divorced husband and his wife might deliver their offering and make restitution for any damage they had caused. Moreover, a promise related to the atoning sacrifice was made, and the contrite in heart undoubtedly often fully met this promise:

"...and the priest shall make atonement for the sin which the man has committed, and he shall be forgiven" (Leviticus 4:35).

The Israelites were required to offer sacrifices regularly until Jesus Christ, the true High Priest, came. Now, neither a priest who offers sacrifices nor an altar or holy of holies remains. Sin was finally and effectively eliminated through the one-time sacrifice of Jesus Christ, making Christians truly sinless in God's eyes. However, it should be noted that the Israelites' sin was acknowledged and confessed over the scapegoat who was taken to an uninhabited place.

Confessional sin is obviously an actual sin and not just the delusions of a paranoid conscience. There is a certain mythical cloud of sin that people talk about and affect to deplore, and yet they have no sense of the solid weight and heinousness of their actual iniquity.

Certain grave divorce offenses involving abuse and humiliation that some husbands and wives have committed are likened to crucibles of foaming traitors. Both the husband and the wife will refuse to acknowledge them if they are left alone.

A few divorcing spouses take a great time to reflect on every action of theirs and its consequences. The majority of divorcees are so close to collapse that they feel embarrassed by their behavior. But as it takes two to tango, it is evident that many of the problems that began and led to the divorce may be the fault of both the husband and the wife. Therefore, when a divorced husband and wife confess their sins to God, they should both remember that it was that actual sin - a terrible and fundamentally repulsive grievance that led to their divorce and that it was paid for by Jesus Christ's atoning work.

The type of sin for which Jesus died is acknowledged with remorse and tears, one that makes the heart seep, condemning sin. Every husband and wife going through a divorce should ask for forgiveness rather than try to find an explanation. May the Spirit of God work in the hearts of any couple considering or going through with a divorce to cause them to repent and, if possible, seek reconciliation.

May every repented divorced couple hear from the voice in Jesus' blood and be encouraged by the knowledge that:

"...by virtue of [His] eternal Spirit [His own preexistent divine personality] has offered Himself as an unblemished sacrifice to God, purify our consciences from dead works and lifeless observances to serve the [ever] living God" (Hebrews 9:14).

Saved By Grace, Damned By Race

I want everyone who has ever interacted with a divorcee to stand before their mental image and let the prophet Jonah deliver the sermon. Jonah made such a good theological assertion after attending God's college that:

"...Salvation and deliverance belong to the Lord!" (Jonah 2:9)

In contrast, salvation is a gift from God, whereas damnation is a choice made by man. Since "salvation" is "of the Lord", it is older than creation and hence, older than marriage and divorce.

Everything about salvation is simple, and everything is sublime.

"But to as many as did receive and welcome Him, He gave the authority (power, privilege, right) to become the children of God, that is, to those who believe in (adhere to, trust in, and rely on) His name" (John 1:12).

Accepting Jesus Christ is a special act.

"He came to that which belonged to Him [to His own—His domain, creation, things, world], and they who were His own did not receive Him and did not welcome Him" (John 1:11).

People who receive Jesus Christ are distinct from those who do not, just as white is distinct from black or light is distinct from darkness. They clearly distinguish themselves and others, come out and welcome Him that others would not. Faith in Jesus Christ is the basis for this reception of Him.

"But to as many as did receive and welcome Him, He gave the authority (power, privilege, right) to become the children of God, that is, to those who believe in (adhere to, trust in, and rely on) His name" (John 1:12).

Accepting Jesus Christ brings salvation. Many sincere Christians have attempted to bring a soul to heaven by force, only to drive it to hell in the process. It takes wisdom and tenderness to save souls, especially the soul of a divorcee, just as Jesus Christ did with the Samaritan woman.

When the Samaritan woman and Jesus first met, He noticed that she had a compassionate inclination toward good things; therefore, He eliminated her ignorance. The Samaritan woman had married five husbands.

"For you have had five husbands, and the man you are now living with is not your husband. In this you have spoken truly" (John 4:18).

Yet, Jesus said to her: *"Give Me a drink" (John 4:7)*

I know a few devoted Christians who wouldn't have touched her with a bar of soap. On the other side, they would have gone right past her. But Jesus was also open to receiving from the woman and giving to her. Jesus went on to speak to the woman who was at the well because He desired more from her than just water. He intended to win her heart, and He succeeded in doing so.

Unfortunately, a lot of Christians are guilty of not wanting to reach the divorcee. However, even doing people good all the time is not the best strategy to draw them in; sometimes, it is better to let them do us good. God never expresses resentment toward the innocent spouse who suffers in marriage and divorce. God had to end His marriage by divorcing Himself because Israel violated the marriage bond.

"…salvation is a gift from God, whereas damnation is a choice made by man."

CHAPTER 08
SINGLEHOOD MUST NOT BE SEEN AS UNGODLY

Human talent, intelligence, and technological advancements have made significant contributions to bridging wide gaps. Since the beginning of time, people have been building bridges. In order to decrease distances and cut down on travel time, bridges are built to cross waterways and valleys. The longest bridge in the world is the Danyang-Kunshan Grand Bridge which is part of China's high-speed rail system between Beijing and Shanghai. The Danyang-construction, Kunshan's, which was finished in 2010, took 10,000 contractors four years to complete. It travels 164,800 meters, or around 102.4 miles, in total.

In today's highly technological society, it is never practical to have a river that is too wide to cross or a stream that is too turbulent for construction workers to work to make it possible for people to cross. There is one gulf, nevertheless, that no amount of engineering or human expertise can fully bridge. There is one chasm that every wing has ever been able to cross. It is the gulf that the 10,000 workers who constructed the Danyang-Kunshan Grand Bridge are unable to bridge.

The gulf separates the rest of the world from the world of joy, suffering, loneliness, and agony that many bachelors and bachelorettes endure. There are channels of connection across the many human classes - men, women, married, single, divorced, black, white, rich, and poor - and this is very appropriate given that the fewer class distinctions that exist, the happier everyone would be.

God's original intent was for there to be only one commonwealth so that the prosperity of one class would have been proportionate to the prosperity of all. Nevertheless, the social and spiritual structure has often been inadvertently maintained by protecting one pillar at the expense of another or by glittering the roof while ignoring the foundations.

Society and several churches have drawn the unofficial border between married and unmarried persons so broadly that we may truly say:

"...between us and you there is a great gulf fixed, so that those who want to pass from here to you cannot, nor can those from there pass to us" (Luke 16:26).

Ironically, the single people that society and certain churches reject, humiliate, and isolate are the foundations of marriage structures. In my discussion about single parenthood, I won't try to climb the mountains of single-parent profundity. I shall reserve all discussion of why some people marry while others do not belong to the erudite theologians who have given that topic their undivided study and who know, or at least, believe they know, a great deal about it. Although it is a fascinating topic, this book is not the right place to discuss it because my objective in discussing singlehood is moral and spiritual, not academic.

I never considered myself to have all the expertise necessary for such a monumental task. However, I ask and believe that God will continue to give me wisdom, just as He has done throughout the book, to edify and comfort rather than impress.

In addition, I ask that the Holy Spirit lead all of us - married and single - through the few universal truths in the book that can benefit everyone regardless of their marital status. Finally, I humbly ask that He lead us into peaceful places of reflection.

To Become Single Is A Matter Of Choice

Every human life contains a number of pivotal moments and thought-provoking venues. Some people experience those pivotal moments and thought-provoking venues when they are still boys and girls, and they are visited in conscience and moved in Spirit. Every young man or every young woman comes to a point in their lives where they must make a choice about their future. Blessed are they if they are already Christians at that point because they will be able, by the leading of the Holy Spirit, to make wise choices that will bring them joy for the rest of their life.

Changes in employment and career, moving away from home, getting promoted to better-paying jobs, or suffering significant losses all mark pivotal moments and thought-provoking venues. Birthday celebrations, New Year's, somber cemeteries, or peculiar incidents in one's past have all come to symbolize pivotal moments in life.

How much of life hangs in the balance at that moment when men and women are getting married! The choice of a soul mate (Spouse) may determine the style of that life. The hands and fingers that put on and wear the adorned engagement and wedding gold rings can reveal if ego, Jesus Christ, the world, or God will be a husband's and wife's household's driving force.

Marriage is too often entered into on an impulse. However, if prospective spouses could understand all the good or bad implications of marriage, they would conclude that the elaborate planning - including gowns, tuxedos, limousines, etc. - is nothing more than a request for God's grace and common sense on the matter of marriage.

Many single people have close relationships with married couples who are either content or dissatisfied with their marriage. Other factors may have driven some other singles to establish close bonds with married couples.

Now, I don't have to spend as much time discussing the negative aspects of bad marriages. All throughout the book, I have thrown them in the path. But I don't want the inclination of the unmarried (single) mind to accentuate them in this section of the book.

THE LEGACY OF MARRIED COUPLES

The perfect ability of godly people to influence and impact the lives of others is a lovely thing. Whether we are conscious of it or not, and whether we believe it or not, we leave trails of evidence with every person we interact with. We leave a good or bad legacy with the people we live with or interact with. When Satan went to the Garden of Eden which I compared to humanity's primordial State of consciousness, the evil creature made sure, with his trial, he would destroy all of Eden's beauty.

Satan left a dreadful legacy in the form of a difficult-to-till, brier-and-thorn-filled wasteland. However, Jesus Christ, who embodies righteousness, kindness, and love and work-tirelessly-for-the-happiness-and-welfare-of-others, has left us with a superior legacy. He died and made the legacy good; He resurrected from the dead and is alive to ensure that no Christian would be robbed of the legacy He has left.

Unfortunately, despite having such a lovely legacy as our inheritance, many Christian husbands and wives continue to live in opposition to what Jesus has left behind. Humans, especially those who are single but plan to get married in the future, make the best mental preparations by carefully observing other married couples.

The world's finest university and institution for learning and practicing self-denial, as well as the expression of the spiritual feelings that make up spiritual life, is marriage. A bachelor or bachelorette must be prepared to get married in order to enroll in the University of Marriage. So, when someone begins to experience a desire to be married, it is as if they have enrolled in a marriage-preparation school. When they begin to make conscious efforts, either through observation or reading about marriage in literature, they have enrolled in the grammar school of marriage.

But before a bachelor or bachelorette decides to be married or not, they meet many married couples along the route, such as at their parents' house, church, or place of employment. This is the ideal graduation from grammar school for marriage. God intended for the family, where a child is raised, to serve as the marriage preparatory school. God intends that in the household, a husband and a wife are to instruct their children in the Christ-like manner of marriage and prepare them for the grammar school of marriage so that young bachelors and bachelorettes may graduate and enter the University of Real Marriage in life.

Unfortunately, many husbands and wives hold a Ph.D. in marriage for more than forty years, but they have led many students to receive "F's" in the course called "Marriage". The worst professor a student might have may be a bad lecturer.

When all evidence suggests that a student knows more about the subject than the teacher, a student finds themselves in a bad predicament. Then, they may write countless words in essays that never seem to be marked, and the poor students would typically learn nothing. Such students can almost physically feel the money they have invested in this course is seeping away.

Anyone can call themselves a "Professor", but not everyone who does so is allowed to teach in an academic setting. Many of those horrific "Professors", whether on purpose or mistakenly, have taught terrible lessons about marriage through their lives and behaviors. They have had a terrible impact on the minds of many bachelors and bachelorettes making them despise marriage.

One of God's greatest gifts to mankind is memory, but memory cannot remember something it has never known. It is apparent that a fact or a truth is more likely to stick in the memory in proportion to how strongly it imprints on the mind. What someone, especially a bachelor or bachelorette, remembers the most after observing a relationship, good or terrible, or after listening to a husband-and-wife converse, is the imagery that most strongly imprints their mind.

When a bachelor or bachelorette says: "That is a great marriage, I pray God to give me its kind", their memory complies with their request. And records the statement on their tablets regardless of whether they write it down in their diary or on their iPad. Sadly, if the remark is: "If this is what they call marriage, then God, I prefer to be single", the memory will also comply in the same way. Because of this, it is important for husbands and wives who share a home with their children to exercise caution in their romantic and conjugal relationships. And more broadly, even though many married couples selfishly don't care how their relationships and lives affect other people, they leave a legacy that will eventually be referenced — whether positively or negatively — without their permission. Because an influence that is established on a bachelor, bachelorette, or anyone else in a strong and lasting fashion will last for generations and be remembered.

And more significantly, they will stand before God one day to answer for how they used the gift of marriage that He gave them. And praise be to God for giving us the gift of a private conscience that keeps us from perpetuating and continuing many of the negative legacies that others have left in our lives and the world.

"For as many as are led by the Spirit of God, these are sons of God." (Romans 8:14).

Marriage Is Meant For The "Converted"

We should not always presume that a bachelor or bachelorette who wants to get married is prepared because they can be acting out of pressure or just for fun. But if they are yearning to enter that significant life stage for the right reasons, we can see from many experiences that they are right with God not only in their thoughts but also in their faith and in their love.

"Now the Lord God said, It is not good (sufficient, satisfactory) that the man should be alone; I will make him a helper (suitable, adapted, complementary) for him" (Genesis 2:18).

The marriage ceremony between a Christian bride and bridegroom is not intended to lead sinners to the saving knowledge of Jesus Christ. It is not intended to specifically guide the man and woman to salvation. However, it is meant for Christians who have previously been saved and converted to enter into a second conversion known as "Holy matrimony".

It is fair to argue that marriages between Christians and non-Christians do occur for a variety of reasons that I have covered in prior chapters. In such marriages, we can see the effect that Christians' virtuous behavior and solemn impressions have made on the unconverted spouse in bringing them to repentance and faith in Jesus Christ.

We must always keep in mind that God operates according to His own will; He instructed Hosea, His prophet, to wed a harlot.

"And the LORD said to Hosea, Go take unto thee a wife of whoredoms and children of whoredoms:" (Hosea 1:2 KJV).

In situations like those, God, who sees the unconverted spouse's heart, ignores their current major fault, and even then, God worked in accordance with the sovereignty of His divine mercy. Yet, this is no excuse for a godly Christian bachelor or bachelorette venturing to parade the world to convert an unbeliever and marry.

I return to where I was after sharing this clear admonition. Marriage to me is like coming to the Lord's table during Communion; every bachelor and bachelorette has to examine themselves as clearly stated in the words below.

"But let every man examine himself, and so let him eat of that bread, and drink of that cup." (1 Corinthians 11:28 KJV).

I do not mean to imply that a bachelor or a bachelorette should conduct such an in-depth self-examination that they determine they are not eligible to get married and leave, feeling completely undeserving of such a noble and glorious gift and honor. A bachelor or a bachelorette should examine themselves with the strong hope and desire that the spouse they have chosen would be on their team and accompany them all the way to the finish line in the marriage race. Neither the bachelor nor the bachelorette should allow the examination to get so dreary and depressing that they almost start looking for reasons to suspect themselves.

However, as it is common in many marriages, a prospective husband and wife should permit their examination in order to properly enter the institution of marriage. People can enter into marriage with the appropriate attitude and never feel forced to leave after a few months or years if they give it great thought and examination.

THE TWO SOLEMN CEREMONIES

Marriage and the Lord's Communion are both solemn ceremonies; which is why I compare the two. And just as Apostle Paul encourages everyone who takes Communion to examine themselves, it is essential for everyone who desires to participate in marriage to do the same in order to do it most solemnly. And undoubtedly, it also means that each and every communicant of marriage, including bachelors and bachelorettes, must come with the utmost humility, as the outcome of any honest examination of oneself must be profound spiritual deliberation.

The examination's other intended outcome is that every bachelor and bachelorette will be able to enter into marriage with knowledge and understanding of why they married, why they have to marry, and on what basis they marry. Among many other things, the consent of the two who intend to marry is required to establish a marriage. Consent is considerably more than simply accepting someone as a husband or wife in accordance with social norms. It involves accepting the husband-and-wife union on the grounds and foundations of Christian marriage. And it is through an introspective examination that the two individuals who intend to get married come to a consensus regarding the marriage.

The Divine law states that relationships have specific obligations and privileges to which both the bachelor and the bachelorette must give their approval. They do not casually agree to share a home, have the benefits and privileges they want, do the chores they want, and otherwise, live as they please. The bachelor and the bachelorette, who were strangers, also chose to live together. Marriage is a Divine ordinance, and the Divine law forbids its modification. A bachelor and the bachelorette must be embraced or refused in its whole. So, if a bachelor and bachelorette examine themselves, they will each understand the actual hunger of their souls and determine whether they are each the suitable food to be fed.

The agreement of a godly marriage consists of a man and a woman living together in accordance with God's ordinance as He has established, and also abiding fully and unconditionally by God's laws about marriage. In the Christian world, real and sincere consent to enter the holy state of matrimony and to dwell therein in accordance with God's rule is required for a marriage to be considered legitimate. This calls for examination, which is even more important given that internal consent dictates the kind and circumstances of an exterior marriage.

Many bachelors and bachelorettes go ahead and consent to perform all of the commitments of the State or Country they live in without undergoing a serious examination or receiving the grace that, in better circumstances, would have helped in doing so. Such a situation in a solemn marriage makes the marriage weak and, more likely than not, exposes the couple to significant temptations.

Marriage is a serious commitment, but it is also quite pleasurable. Any bachelor or bachelorette, as well as married couples, who have followed God's commandments, will admit that it was difficult to follow all of the restrictions, but the rewards are always glorious.

"The disciples said to Him, If the case of a man with his wife is like this, it is neither profitable nor advisable to marry" (Matthew 19:10).

The character of Jesus Christ is so beautifully infused with the perfection of His nature. He displayed a perfect character while still a Man. However, no one can very readily tell where His meekness merges with His bravery and where His beauty merges with His boldness. When He once provided marriage counseling, He acknowledged the difficulties but just stated that not all men could understand the statement. Jesus Christ did not make the marriage laws more lenient as stated in Matthew 19:10.

"The disciples said to Him, If the case of a man with his wife is like this, it is neither profitable nor advisable to marry."

If Jesus did not feel the need to change marriage and its rules, then it cannot be changed. Averagely, very few people - rich or poor, attractive or unattractive, short or tall - have ever reached the age of thirty-five without having had, at least, one opportunity to be married. However, every godly, intelligent person would choose to live single rather than commit their lives to a man or woman they do not respect and love. Any Christian man or woman should not enter into marriage impulsively or casually. A bachelor and a bachelorette should enter marriage respectfully, confidentially, wisely, and maturely, just as we do when we take the Lord's Communion.

In the summer of 2019, UN Women published a report stating that single life is on the rise and marriage is declining globally. "Families in a Changing World…" A part of being honest is admitting that many people other than Christians have long chosen to remain single, such as Apostle Paul and the fathers and nuns of the Roman Catholic Church. They have opted to remain single for a variety of reasons, including their strong religious beliefs and the complexity of the marriage that rules them.

Having Access To Marriage Blessings

God's blessing is necessary for a happy marriage because He is the wellspring of the couple's spiritual life, as well as their marriage. The blessings of God are the mechanism by which He unites the man and the woman and makes them into one, nurtures them, and keeps them together so that the man and the woman are inseparable.

In every Christian marriage, God - not man - truly marries the couple, just as God - not man - truly administers every Christian sacrament even though He does so through man.

Christian sacraments and Christian marriage, both, owe their effectiveness and holiness to the role that God plays in them. That is why a bachelor and a bachelorette have to examine themselves just as a Christian does before taking Communion. This puts the onus of upholding the marriage on God first and then on the man and the woman who choose to get married.

Unfortunately, because a premarital examination is overlooked and couples hastily consider marriage and enter it, the temporary and long-term joy of one or both of the husband and the wife involved is often ruined:

"But let every man examine himself, and so let him eat…" (1 Corinthians 11:28 KJV).

Paul did not say that "Let the parent examine himself for the child" or "Let a friend examine themselves for a friend." No! He says: "Let a man examine himself, and so let him eat." Or I say: "Let a man and woman examine themselves before they marry."

An examination of marriage in light of God and His law makes the prospective husband and wife meditate upon the person of Jesus Christ. In every holy ordinance, like the Lord's Supper and in this context, marriage, everything depends upon the right understanding of them. There is no efficacy in water, whether it is applied by immersion or by aspersion; the value of the ordinance depends upon the conviction that the Christian has when we are baptized, that it is the will of our Savior Jesus Christ that we should, thus, confess His faith.

There is nothing efficacious in that small bread or the wine; the bread has no more virtue in it than there is in any other bread at Costco and BJ's bakery section. The wine is, in itself, no more a means of grace than any other wine that ever was pressed out from a vintage in a village. It is the thought that shall be excited by that bread and that wine that will be the benefit; it is the mind seeing through the visible sign that is inwardly signified. Hence, it is that Jesus Christ calls every prospective spouse to the same self-examination that their intellect may be stirred, and their mind prepared, under the influence of the Divine law and Spirit, to understand the meaning of marriage to which they commit themselves.

No priest of a church or no clerk in a courthouse can give a man and a woman a certificate that really entitles them to receive the blessings of God on their marriage. In their offices as priests, they are privileged to see men and women marry in their churches. But, by so doing, they never mean to imply that they, thereby, certify that the man and woman are really fit for the marriage blessings of God.

That is a matter which must rest with each man and woman because sadly, many people stand before a priest to exchange marriage vows and proclaim they "Know nothing why they should not be joined in holy matrimony" when they may have been sleeping around and may be five months or so pregnant. The priest represents God to officiate the marriage, but He cannot compel God to bless a marriage; so, a bachelor and a bachelorette have to "examine" themselves.

If they are wise, they will also base their choices on the results of their own examination of themselves in God's eyes, which will guide them in determining what to do and what not to do. Many husbands and wives have carried a burden on their consciences for many years that they did not mean to shoulder because they entered into a marriage in the wrong way. They can be reluctant to acknowledge that their actions have prevented them from receiving the Divine assistance that is necessary to carry the burden.

According to the commonly used definition of the word "sacrament", marriage is not one. However, if someone refuses to acknowledge it as such just like the cross and all other Christian sacraments, it will not be able to convey the Divine blessing to those who regard it lightly or to those who disregard it.

Taking the Word of God as their guide, the prospective husband and wife should judge themselves to be Christians, and therefore, they will adhere to all the laws of God about marriage.

Marriage And Communion Are, In Principle, Alike

Many people express their contempt for marriage which God has blessed and given to humanity. The Lord's Supper and Baptism are two ordinances that Christians are familiar with as being established by Jesus Christ. Many Christians despise and reject the idea of marriage as a sacrament because they are only familiar with the two ordinances that are depicted in the Bible. Given that it was ordained by God and is the most sacred union a man and a woman can have, marriage is one of the most significant and holy ordinances.

The Communion that Jesus Christ instituted has a very solemn and emotional quality to it since it is specifically about Himself. Other symbols illustrate the truths that Jesus preached, the blessings He obtained, or the tasks and commissions He commanded. But the central focus of Communion is on Jesus Christ.

In keeping with His habit of speaking in parables, Jesus Christ portrayed Himself in one parable as a bachelor whose Father was willing to honor Him with a marriage ceremony. Jesus talked of a king who wanted to show His Son the utmost honor.

"But they were not concerned and paid no attention [they ignored and made light of the summons, treating it with contempt] and they went away - one to his farm, another to his business" (Matthew 22:5).

His Son deserved to be treated with honor; thus, He was a perfect Son and, the Father, a loving Father. The King is, doubtless, God, the Father who delights to honor Jesus, His Only-begotten Son. The Father loves the Son with whom He is one. The Son has deserved well at the Father's hands, for He has been:

"*…obedient unto death, even the death of the cross.*" *(Philippians 2:8 KJV).*

It is the Father's aim in the work of grace to glorify His Son who, as God and man in one nature, is the channel of grace to fallen men. He proposes to do this now that the Lord Jesus takes His church into marriage union with Himself. The incarnate God calls a chosen company, the bride, the Lamb's wife and celebrates, thus, early in the day, this happy union with a wedding breakfast to which He invites multitudes to come.

It is a feast of mercy, grace, and peace, a marriage feast of delight and joy. The feast is for the glorifying of the Lord Jesus Christ in a very special manner. But before Jesus Christ could be honored by the Father with the marriage ceremony, He had to be obedient by honoring all the laws relating to His marriage to His spouse. Jesus could not consummate the marriage relationship before they set a date for the marriage ceremony. Although God, He learned obedience and endured all shame until He received His Father's blessing on His and His wife's marriage.

Although there are others who dishonor Him by turning down the invitation and others who come in improper clothing, it is not the subject of my attention. My emphasis is on the marriage blessings' giver and recipient. The entire parable contains a lot of gems. And it is simple to see its spiritual significance.

There are many key details in the Bible that illustrate that Jesus Christ is the church's bridegroom. And each one can be analogized to have a deeper and more illuminating meaning.

Obedience To The Core For The Blessings Of God

Because Jesus Christ likens His relationship to the church to a marriage relationship and, thus, a Divine ordinance, it is important to follow His every step by which He married His wife and received Divine blessings.

Failing to understand the meaning of the marriage ordinance, people have, at least, occasionally, rendered marriages worthless. However, in order that husbands and wives understand what they are doing and the spiritual significance of the picture-based marriage instruction that Jesus Christ established in the Communion and will continue to do so until the end of the age, He reminded His Church of His extremely large cross sacrifice which was motivated by love.

An unsuitable condition of mind or heart will cause harm to a man and a woman who choose not to honor the Divine Ordinances of Marriage and receive Divine Blessings. Their worth is based on the Divine institution, as well as the faith of the husband and the wife who receive them. Although the institution is Divine, it was never intended for it to function solely through the exercise of Divine power without human involvement.

Unless it obtains life from the Divine blessing in each specific circumstance, it is merely a form. A husband and a wife who seek it in a pure state of mind and heart will never be denied that blessing. It is never given to a husband and a wife who are in a mental state where they do not deserve it.

An opus operatum, or a work created by divine force without human approval, does not exist among the Divine ordinances. The disposition of the heart and the mind in which the commandment is accepted determines the degree of the blessing. The most abhorrent of all abominations is the concept of sponsors, whether in salvation or the Lord's Supper. No priest, no parent, no spouse, nor any friend may sponsor anyone; each must appear before God on their own.

Let us imagine Priest Solomon was a close friend of Stephen who was a member of his church. And Stephen was sexually weak; therefore, he slept around. Priest Solomon, instead of admonishing Stephen to abstain from fornication, honestly promised the latter that he (Solomon) will uphold God's holy commandments for his church member. So, Stephen was still free to live his life in violation of the rules of the Lord's Communion. But on communion day, Stephen could still come and take part in the Communion. In that case, Stephen may participate in the Lord's Supper externally, yet, no interior effect would be generated, or worse, only negative effects would occur.

The beneficial effect of Communion would be lost since Stephen did not genuinely seek after it and did not satisfy the prerequisites for its granting. In such situations, Stephen participated in the Lord's Supper on an exterior level without reaping the advantages internally.

Therefore, there are two types of Communions: inward and outward. Without the outward, the inward cannot exist. The outward, however, may exist independently of the inward; in which case, it loses all spiritual significance and true value. However, since no one knows the heart, and that is where the problem is, man cannot contest the legitimacy of the outward ceremony.

When it comes to marriage, if Bismarck and Silvia choose to disobey or go against God's laws of marriage, they may have a valid outside marriage but not a true inside marriage. No one can contest their marriage's legality. It is a marriage that is legal under both divine and human law in all ways that a man is capable of understanding. It will be respected by families, friends, the church, the State, and society as well. The church is composed of finite beings just like the State and society, finite beings can only see what is on the outside. However, God, who sees the innermost parts of people, may see that there has been no consent to a genuine Christian marriage, no divine blessing, no indissoluble bond between Bismarck and Silvia, and no sanctity of the marriage. The marriage of Bismarck and Silvia may not have been permitted by God's law, and as a result, the marriage may not be legitimate. All of that might be accurate, regardless of the procedures used to consummate the marriage.

The irrevocable marriage and Bismarck's power will exist, but none of the conditions that make marriage a blessing will, and they will be seen as unbearable frustrations. In the case of Bismarck and Silvia, the priest's blessing - a symbol from the outside world or a specific way to celebrate is not necessary for the Divine blessing to occur.

No matter what form it takes, marriage and the sanctity that is part of its core can exist. However, this cannot happen without internal consent that is expressed through activity outside of the marriage that complies with the law. God, thus, bestows His blessings in response to such consent.

If Bismarck and Silvia have already broken God's law, it is not in the power of anyone - not, even, a priest - to grant them the right to enjoy His blessings. It is up to the two to seek God in prayer and repent of their sins. "Let a man examine himself."

"The disposition of the heart and the mind in which the commandment is accepted determines the degree of the blessing."

CHAPTER 09

THE FLESH DISHONORS MARRIAGE

Augustine constantly prays: "Lord, deliver me from that evil man, myself." The flesh is every human's worst enemy, but notably that of the unmarried. The Holy Spirit, on the other hand, is everyone's best friend and the Person who loves us the most. The Holy Spirit dwells within every child of God in a manner similar to how He did so while the Son of God, Jesus Christ, was on earth. The Holy Spirit resides in our fallen and unfinished cleansed manhood while Jesus lived in perfect manhood of His own.

Jesus lived in a human body and had complete power over it. But regrettably, the Holy Spirit has to strive to control us because despite His dominion over our hearts, there remains an evil spirit that is firmly embedded in our bodies and is determined to bring trouble.

"For the desires of the flesh are opposed to the [Holy] Spirit, and the [desires of the] Spirit are opposed to the flesh (godless human nature); for these are antagonistic to each other [continually withstanding and in conflict with each other], so that you are not free but are prevented from doing what you desire to do" (Galatians 5:17).

God refers to the sin of idolatry as fornication throughout the Old Testament because it is the turning away from the love that should be directed toward the true God. That love, when is given in favor of other gods, defiles the idolater's heart which is a sin against God.

The whole history of the human race is a record of the wars of God against idolatry. His right hand has dashed in pieces the enemy and cast the ancient idols to the ground.

"For they provoked Him to [righteous] anger with their high places [for idol worship] and moved Him to jealousy with their graven images. When God heard this, He was full of [holy] wrath; and He utterly rejected Israel, greatly abhorring and loathing [her ways]" (Psalm 78:58-59).

With what indignation, then, must God look down upon that harlot, adulterous person, or those fornicators when they are infatuated in all their sanctuaries and sleep with countless men and women? What fury, then, must God feel when He looks down on those adulterous fornicators who play the harlot in their sanctuaries and have untold men and women sleep with them? Such actions by humans are PROMISCUOUS and a mockery of love. The term "love", which is a gift from heaven, is trampled upon by promiscuity which breeds impure passion and repulsive burning desire. Everywhere and forever, promiscuous sex has been seen as unlawful. There has never been a group of people proven to be so barbaric as to willfully ignore the value of morality in possession of particular women by particular men. Apostle Paul addressed the Corinthian church in the clearest possible terms.

"For I am zealous for you with a godly eagerness and a divine jealousy, for I have betrothed you to one Husband, to present you as a chaste virgin to Christ" (2 Corinthians 11:2).

Paul was eager, cautious, and cautiously concerned for their holiness so that Jesus Christ could be honored in their lives. It is little less than outright blasphemy against the purity of love to speak of "love" when a man covets his neighbor's wife or when a woman disobeys the law:

"You shall not commit adultery" (Exodus 20:14).

Sexual relations with someone you are not married to are an act of lust, not love; lust is the devil's gift, not God's. The unbelieving world hardly ever criticizes "fornication" but Christianity is most vehement in its condemnation of it. Fornication and adultery constantly taint domestic life, and when the marriage covenant and ordinance are broken, it degrades the glories of the marriage.

When wives, husbands, bachelors, and bachelorettes talk about Christianity while breaking their marriage vows and virginity, they expose blatant hypocrisy. Every act of fornication and adultery is a sin that as much says:

"I do not acknowledge God to be the owner of my body; I will do as I please with it."

Every time a married person engages in extramarital sex or an unmarried person engages in intercourse with anyone; they use foul language that actually means:

"My body is my own; it is not the temple of the Holy Spirit."

Human nature's wandering after evil and lust for what is prohibited leads to attempts to remove God from power and set Satan in His place. The fornicator and adulterer use the argument: *"Who is God to tell me what to do with my body?"* It is a calculated violation of God's dignity, an attack on His majesty, and an insult to His kingdom.

Fornicating or committing adultery by a Christian is an act of rebellion. Such so-called Christians have rebellion engraved on their foreheads - presumptuous sins because they hear the Word every day and still reject the purity and follow adultery and fornication despite having an enlightened conscience and knowing better.

In these immoral times, however, some people have emerged who view fornication, adultery, and promiscuity as minor sins and even strive to use the law to make it safer to practice a crime that undermines the foundation of a healthy marriage. It is a horrible sign of the times; even the pagans decried such immorality; Christians must not put up with it.

Prayer Is Inevitable In Purity

In this universe, there is a war between two powers. One is the power of good, whose ruler is God, and the other is the power of evil, which is embodied by Satan, the Prince of the power of the air. And the Holy Spirit, who is well aware of the specifics of the ongoing war, took up much more room in the bible to write down Jesus Christ's petitions as He draws closer to the end of His earthly ministry.

Jesus dedicated Himself entirely to prayer after the Last Supper since His public ministry was over, and there was nothing left to do but to be arrested and be crucified. In the time that was left before He would give His life, Jesus prepared Himself for specific intercession.

Even though He wasn't actively preaching to the crowds or healing the sick as He had previously done, Jesus Christ continuously poured out His soul in prayers before He poured it out to death. In one such incident of Jesus' intercessory petitions, He fervently asks the Father for an immeasurable blessing. He begins by asking:

"...*Holy Father, keep in Your Name in the knowledge of Yourself those whom You have given Me...*" *(John 17:11).*

Jesus then repeats:

"*I do not ask that You will take them out of the world, but that You will keep and protect them from the evil one*" *(John 17:15).*

Yet, the request for protection against evil is insufficient: Jesus calls out,

"*Sanctify them [purify, consecrate, separate them for Yourself, make them holy] by the Truth; Your Word is Truth*" *(John 17:17).*

Jesus Christ, indeed, wants His disciples to be holy in a good way. I would not be able to follow the term "sanctify" through all of its semantic variations, but one or two will have to do. First, it implies devoting oneself to someone's service as that is clearly the meaning of the term later on in the sentence.

"*And so for their sake and on their behalf I sanctify (dedicate, consecrate) Myself, that they also may be sanctified (dedicated, consecrated, made holy) in the Truth.*" *(John 17:19).*

Jesus was without sin; hence, sanctification does not apply to Him because He has not been cleansed of sin. Both His deeds and character were free of sin. Jesus' prayer had a number of different meanings, but one of them was that He would have every Christian dedicated to God, accepted, and appointed for heavenly purposes.

Christians are not of this world; instead, we were bought with the blood of Jesus. So, we are His through whom the debt is settled. We are Jesus' property, and He offers us to His Father, pleading with Him to accept us and sanctify us for His purposes.

Jesus advises us not to get married to unbelievers or be unequally yoked with same and any other evil act because we are sanctified. Thus, a Christian must stop following the crowd in sins like fornication, adultery, gossip, thievery, etc.

In my opinion, the second portion of Jesus' prayer is a call for Christians to be holy and pure. I have always maintained that the bible should be interpreted in accordance with common sense. Thus, I will say that the message of Jesus Christ - along with His love, good deeds, and intercessory prayers - is unmistakably a command:

"I have asked the Father to preserve and sanctify you so be holy."

Jesus does defer to logic. His ministry often displays grace. He does persuade people through persuasive arguments and power. He invites us and gently woos us to be wise.

SINGLEHOOD IS A WORK-IN-PROGRESS

In a way, Jesus' invitation to all of humanity and His ministry for humanity - including Salvation - are divided into two sections. Everybody who believes in Jesus Christ is saved completely and without the need for any effort on their side because "It is finished" and we are whole in Him. However, there are two aspects to our Salvation, one of which is finished and the other of which is still unfinished but will eventually be finished. Work for us makes up the first portion of our Salvation, and work in us makes up the second. No one can improve upon God's wonderful work of Salvation for us. Jesus Christ has entirely atoned for all the sins of His people. The benefit goes to:

"... one who, not working [by the Law], trusts (believes fully) in Him Who justifies the ungodly, his faith is credited to him as righteousness (the standing acceptable to God)" (Romans 4:5).

"But to one who, not working [by the Law], trusts (believes fully) in Him Who justifies the ungodly, his faith is credited to him as righteousness (the standing acceptable to God)". (Romans 4:5).

Justification comes from God's free gift rather than any human effort. The second stage of Salvation entails God the Holy Ghost performing work within us. The Holy Spirit enters a man during rebirth and gives them a new nature. However, He does not obliterate the old which remains still to be dealt with and overcome. The nature that the Holy Spirit imbues is perfect in kind and degree, but it is not perfect in its growth. It is like a seed that needs to develop into a tree or a baby that needs to mature into a perfect man's stature. The components of total perfection are present in the new nature, but they need to be brought out and, in the words of the scripture,

"...work out (cultivate, carry out to the goal, and fully complete) your own salvation with reverence and awe and trembling (self-distrust, with serious caution, tenderness of conscience, watchfulness against temptation, timidly shrinking from whatever might offend God and discredit the name of Christ)." (Philippians 2:12).

After being incorporated by God, it is now the responsibility of the Christian life to fully implement the hidden underlying principle until the whole system is affected.

Holiness Without Which No Christian Can Enjoy A Heaven-Made Marriage

In the same way, there are two parts to Salvation, there are two sides to holiness. However, many people often argue that there is only one king, which is the imputed holiness of Jesus Christ.

"Strive to live in peace with everybody and pursue that consecration and holiness without which no one will ever see the Lord" (Hebrews 12:14).

Jesus requires Christians to strive or pursue holiness just as we should strive for peace. And it must be obvious to any intelligent man that pursuing holiness is something that belongs to the act and responsibility of the one who pursues it. Christians are expected to pursue actual peace - not the kind that Jesus has made just for us, but rather the kind that produces the fruits of righteousness that are sown in the peace of those who pursue peace.

"And the effect of righteousness will be peace [internal and external], and the result of righteousness will be quietness and confident trust forever "(Isaiah 32:17).

Christians are also expected to uphold holiness which must be demonstrated in practice and it is the antithesis of impurity.

"For God did not call us to uncleanness, but in holiness" (1 Thessalonians 4:7).

If we take Jesus Christ's holiness as a giving, it is not something to follow. That is something we already possess; Jesus Christ gives His holiness to us in the instant we believe. Because it is conferred upon our soul at the moment it embraces Jesus Christ, we do not pursue such holiness. However, the other kind of holiness is the practical, vital holiness which is the purport of God's admonition. It is in conformity to the will of God and obedience to His command. That holiness is, in fine, the Holy Spirit's work in the soul, by which a person is made like God and becomes a partaker of the divine nature, being delivered from the corruption which is in the world through lust, fornication, adultery, etc.

Now, if Jesus were to require perfect holiness from Christians, without which no one could have any fellowship with Him, He would exclude His own mother, Mary, whom the angel said (was highly favored). Since no one genuinely understands, their own hearts will ever claim to possess even a small amount of holiness of their own. We are grateful to Jesus for requesting holiness without the use of an adjective rather than holiness perfected.

Christians must work to progress in their pursuit of holiness. That type of holiness is embryonic when it first appears in the soul as a mustard seed, similar to the new nature at rebirth. It could be anything that is yearning, gasping for, wanting, or striving for in the heart rather than something that has been fully achieved.

The mustard seed will grow until it becomes a tree as the Holy Spirit waters it. In a heart that has undergone regeneration, holiness is still a baby; it has not yet grown up. It is perfect in every way, but it has not yet reached its full potential.

The presence of various flaws in ourselves should not lead us to conclude that we lack holiness. We should aim at holiness instead. Thus, despite our flaws, we should not resist holiness. Whether Christians or nonbelievers like it or not, Jesus' mandate about holiness is still valid. Some people, married and unmarried, have a personal, self-explanatory aversion to holiness, just as no thief has ever had any fondness for a policeman, soldier, or judge. Yet, their holiness stands, and it means no other than what it says:

"Without Holiness, No One Can Enjoy a Heaven Made Marriage." Solomon says:

"For the word of a king is authority and power, and who can say to him, What are you doing? (Ecclesiastes 8:4).

Mary, A Perfect Example Of Singlehood

Many people have the name Mary, but one Mary stands out because of the title that has been given to her. As different names are given to different people to distinguish them from others with the same name, such as Jacob being called Israel and Abraham is called the Friend of God or Father of the Faithful, so, too, is this Mary satisfactorily distinguished by that infallible companion to her name, THE VIRGIN.

Joseph, the reputed Father of Jesus Christ, and Mary were engaged to be married. Unbeknownst to him; however, God had chosen his virgin fiancée from among all the daughters of Eve to stand as the focal point of a miracle. The Holy Spirit overshadowed Mary, she got pregnant, and gave birth to Jesus Christ, the Godman who is the Savior of the world" (Holy Ghost). With surprising uniformity, certain religious believers believe that the mother of Jesus remained a virgin until her death, even after giving birth.

But in this context of my writing, I am referring to the Mary the Bible reports that her first-born was Jesus the Son of God, and James, Joses, Juda, and Simon and daughters.

"Is not this the Carpenter, the son of Mary and the brother of James and Joses and Judas and Simon? And are not His sisters here among us? And they took offense at Him and were hurt [that is, they disapproved

of Him, and it hindered them from acknowledging His authority] and they were caused to stumble and fall" (Mark 6:3).

The name of Mary, the highly Favored, is a name full of joy, grace, love, and self-sacrifice. The Virgin Mother was honored among women. Understandably, Christians have not always treated Mary with the reverence she merits because we're so determined to avoid any superstitious worship of her. And for a good reason - any informed mind should find such superstition repugnant

"You shall have no other gods before or besides Me" (Exodus 20:3).

However, it does not follow that Mary suffers as a result of the uproar after we have endured it: Instead, we honor the memories of that virtuous woman. The words of the angel Gabriel were true and compelling:

"...Hail, O favored one endued with grace]! The Lord is with you! Blessed (favored of God) are you before all other women!" (Luke 1:28).

Mary was also right when she said:

"...For behold, from now on all generations [of all ages] will call me blessed and declare me happy and to be envied!" (Luke 1:48).

The reason we say so is that she was, in fact, blessed. Mary was the most honorable and deserving woman because she was the ever-blessed Mother of God. The names of Mary's parents were Joachim and Anne. And she had a cousin called Elizabeth who was married to Zachariah, the high priest.

And in biblical times, a parent might choose a baby's name based on events surrounding the conception (as in the case of Isaac) or delivery (as in the case of Jacob and Benjamin, Jabez), occasionally from divine acts or attributes like Jesus Christ.

As it is customary for Jews, eight days following the birth of the Blessed Baby, a religious and social event was going be conducted in Joachim and Anne's home to name the newborn child. To support this event, many customs and prayers was going be held. Like the story of John the Baptist's naming, it's conceivable that during the baby's naming ceremony at Mary's parents' home, guests gave Joachim and Anne a list of names for the child from among the names of their numerous and esteemed ancestors.

Nevertheless, like John the Baptist, God intended to use the newborn baby to bring Salvation to the pagan. Hence, Joachim and Anne, like Elizabeth and Zachary, ended all these courteous recommendations by introducing Mary, a name that had never been used in the family.

Look Beyond The External

When I observe the parallel and mystifying events in the lives of Hannah, an adult married woman, and Mary, a young virgin, I feel compelled to repeatedly emphasize how differently but superficially similar life treats mankind.

The two lives imply a parallel between two facts that God intends to establish; Hannah's life is a fact He occasionally permits, and Mary's life is a fact He purposefully instills. The two lives of the women are a subject more suited to private reflection than to public expression or explanation alone. Though it must be felt, it is never possible to express.

Who can describe Hannah's joy when she gave birth to Samuel after everything she went through at the hands of her rival Peninnah?

Who in this world is able to describe Mary's joy in giving birth to God? Who knows how she felt when someone shouted: "There goes the mother of the Savior of the world" as she walked by?

How should we express Hannah's suffering when she tried everything humanly possible to have a child but was unsuccessful? Nobody can tell or even conceive what she moaned in the harem.

What language should we use to describe Mary's suffering as she stood at the cross, heard her Son Jesus sob, and He addressed her after everything He had gone through:

"...Dear woman, See, [here is] your son!" (John 19:26).

At one point in their lives, both women and maybe their spouses had a sorrowful spirit. A sorrowful spirit is unattractive on its own. The majority of bachelors and bachelorettes don't think twice about expressing their dislike of miserable people. They only desire to be in the company of a bachelor or a bachelorette who has a lively eyeball, a cheerful smile, a vibrant demeanor, and a kind tone.

They simply want a husband and a wife who can, at least, provide them with such serene composure. Those people are only drawn to bachelors and bachelorettes who have a calm enjoyment that permeates the atmosphere and makes home joyful so that they will always be filled with joy and laughter. There are bachelors and bachelorettes, married people and divorcees, who ought to display more of such cheerful graces than they already do. And they deserve a lot of blame for their spitefulness, cruelty, and annoyance. But I have no doubt that there are other bachelors and bachelorettes out there who try their hardest to embody all that is delightful but fall short because, like Hannah and Mary, they have a sorrowful spirit and are unable to let go of the sorrow that weighs on their hearts.

It is useless to tell the night to shine as brightly as the day or to tell winter snow to wear summer wildflowers just as it is useless to correct a sorrowful heart. A dog or an elephant cannot soar through the air like a bird.

Due to the suffering they have endured at the hands of certain persons they believed to be Christians, some incredibly godly people find it difficult to be joyful; they are sorrowful. However, well-priced things appear in the grieving spirits of many bachelors, bachelorettes, husbands, and wives just like Hannah and Mary.

Many people possess actual godliness just like the two women do; they are godly men and women. The sincerity of Hannah and Mary's hearts toward God is unequivocally attested to in the bible. The sincerity and ubiquity of the prayers of the two women cannot be questioned. We have no reason to question the integrity of Hannah and Mary's holy joy, their firmness of faith, or the enthusiasm of their devotion in their songs preserved in the bible.

"Hannah prayed, and said, My heart exults and triumphs in the Lord; my horn (my strength) is lifted up in the Lord. My mouth is no longer silent, for it is opened wide over my enemies, because I rejoice in Your salvation". (1Samuel 2:1).

"And Mary said, My soul magnifies and extols the Lord, And my spirit rejoices in God my Savior, For He has looked upon the low station and humiliation of His handmaiden. For behold, from now on all generations [of all ages] will call me blessed and declare me happy and [aa]to be envied!" (Luke 1:46-48).

The two women were exceptionally gracious people who feared God more than most people, yet they were "sorrowful".

Many Christians make the same instantaneous assumption that certain Hannahs are drunk, crazy, and unforgiving just like Eli did.

"Eli said to her, How long will you be intoxicated? Put wine away from you" (1 Samuel 1:14).

It is very human for us to avoid drawing the conclusion that God doesn't love the person who endues sadness. We may more safely reason in the opposite direction because a person's spiritual state cannot be accurately determined by his or her external surroundings.

VIRGINITY AND CELIBACY ADD TO A SUCCESSFUL MARRIAGE

The virginity and celibacy of Mary, Joseph, and many others in our world, who followed in their footsteps before getting married, make me remember that everyone can be whatever God wants them to be. Virginity and abstinence are the delicate, pure, and wonderful jewels for which marriage prepares the participants.

The world opposes the idea of celibacy and virginity prior to marriage; yet, God demands it of all of His children since it is one of the most attractive building blocks of Christian marriage. There is no law of God that promotes or forbids permanent celibacy. However, celibacy is in agreement with God's most intimate and delicate desire.

Even while the practice of perpetual celibacy is fraught with serious challenges, it offers a wealth of spiritual guidance. Only once did Jesus Christ express a desire for people to permanently maintain their celibacy. He refrained from doing it again and instead waited for His Spirit to be poured out on all flesh to allow God's gift to reach human souls.

Then Paul, in his writing to the Corinthians, said:

"You were bought with a price [purchased with a preciousness and paid for by Christ]; then do not yield yourselves up to become [in your own estimation] slaves to men [but consider yourselves slaves to Christ]. So, brethren, in whatever station or state or condition of life each one was when he was called, there let him continue with and close to God. Now concerning the virgins (the marriageable [c]maidens) I have no command of the Lord, but I give my opinion and advice as one who by the Lord's mercy is rendered trustworthy and faithful (1 Corinthians 7:23-25).

In order to encourage celibacy and virginity, Paul speaks continually of the tribulations and cares of this life. Peter was married because we read about his mother-in-law.

"Then He arose and left the synagogue and went into Simon's (Peter's) house. Now Simon's mother-in-law was suffering in the grip of a burning fever, and they pleaded with Him for her" (Luke 4:38).

God, thus, expresses a desire for celibacy rather than a demand and fixes the choice of those who choose to respect the purest flesh of Jesus Christ by bodily virginity. It is sufficient to remark that God does not advocate celibacy which is merely selfish sexual promiscuity.

What keeps people from getting married is not the ordinary chilly and idle chastity but the inexcusable immorality of those unfortunate ones who claim to be able to multiply and diversify their joys without wearing restraints. Even if they avoid upsetting families or seducing moral rectitude, they don't hold back on revealing their scandalous alliances until they are exhausted from their exploits, intoxicated from their revelry, and under the control of a sycophantic woman who will reward them for their misfortune with her slavish obedience.

These individuals of wickedness should be destroyed by human disdain since human laws dare not touch them; they richly deserve it. Along with their unfortunate celibacy, they also surrender to their dreary virginity which neither excuses nature for its unfavorable treatment of it; neither fortune nor the world can be blamed for depriving it of its gifts or for condemning them to a life of endless loneliness through their indifference or contempt.

The sad legacy of wilting elderly women whose passionate marriage aspirations evolve into ill-intentioned grief with age. The only thing their sour spirits can dream of doing in their perfect bodies is getting back at all loveliness, all virtue, all happiness, and the compulsory celibacy they see as a disgrace. These determined liars never stop ruining the best reputations with their toxic lips.

God, who has never desired them, will say to them:

"*... I do not know you*" *(Matthew 25:12).*

The virgins that God chose to know and love are those who have been favored by Him and who, by voluntarily receiving His tender caresses, have been changed into a conduit of grace to the world. Those virgins give birth to the Savior of the World. I have always wondered what would have become of them if Joseph and Mary had been sleeping around yet, pretending to be observing celibacy.

You know how passionate a person is about one thing; when that one thing consumes their entire humanhood, something marvelous is bound to happen. Count on that. The desire in their hearts will manifest itself in some way, especially if they communicate it with God in prayer.

Their celibacy did result in something wonderful. Soon, there was an appointment for Mary and Joseph. Bachelors and bachelorettes, as you submit your bodies to God as living sacrifices but are unable to find the right appointment, keep waiting on God in prayer and fasting. Eventually, your appointment will come your way like a noonday.

A sincere and compassionate heart has never regretted finding a fitting home inside God's marriage institution. Each committed and loving bachelor or bachelorette is required in some capacity inside the God-ordained institution of marriage.

Because the institute has not engaged you, you may feel as though you are delaying and appear to have stood in the marriage institution passively for nothing. But stay there and wait while you pray. Your chance will arrive as your heart is filled with a warm purpose. The hour will need its bachelors and bachelorettes, and if you are ready, you shall not be without your hour as a prospective bride and a groom.

The God who sent Joseph and Mary an opportunity in a way that they could not have expected will send an opportunity to every bachelor and bachelorette. There shall be an opportunity for every Christian who awaits Jesus Christ. My prologue leads to this parenthesis where I discuss the challenges a bachelor and a bachelorette encounter.

CHAPTER 10
WASTED HOURS IN PROMISQUITY

It is usually a great blessing when appetite and food coincide. Many bachelors and bachelorettes are hungry for the marriage feast; but no marriage dinner exists. They require everyone's empathy. Other bachelors and bachelorettes have marriage steak but no appetite; while they may not necessarily beg for our empathy, they unquestionably need it.

Many bachelors and bachelorettes who have converted to Christianity had testified that they had completely lost their appetite after being served so lavishly at the marriage dinner when they were in the world.

When the Israelites were in the wilderness, a metaphor for their conversion from the world to Christianity, they eventually developed such anxiety about eating that even though they were given the bread of heaven and, for a brief period, men actually did eat angel food, they still said:

"...and we loathe this light (contemptible, unsubstantial) manna" (Numbers 21:5).

Unfortunately, there are many bachelors and bachelorettes in the world and in the church who run the risk of contracting the same disease. They consumed their wedding feast earlier than intended, depriving themselves of the finest of delicacies when the time was right. Many of them, including some devout Christians, wasted their morning hours engaging in promiscuity.

When the time came for them to marry, those prospective brides and grooms had the terrible experience of realizing that the greatest part of their day - and even noon - was long gone when they were in their later years. And they only had the evening which was usually only a short one, to properly eat, appreciate, and take pleasure in the marriage dinner. It is regrettable that so many Christian bachelors and bachelorettes purposefully live their lives eating the wedding supper when they should not and forget that they will be unable to directly or indirectly positively impact others. Because of this, many people become just like a faint light on a foggy day when they marry and have children because their guilt prevents them from shining bright enough to illuminate other people's lives.

Many such husbands and wives pick and choose from the marriage buffet as if neither a man nor a woman was right for them, just as they did when they were younger. Those kinds of husbands and wives are, hence, prevalent in the divorce world. Similar to the old gluttons, those men and women demand their spouses exploit the sky, sea, earth, and air for their enjoyment before becoming accustomed to hot sauces and exotic flavors of marriage.

Contrary to common assumption, the truth is that the ideal dish for the steak of marriage is the hunger of marriage. While the pastry chefs and kitchen staff in the marriage institution may use a variety of cuisine processes to prepare delicate dishes for the marriage dinner, God, the institutor of marriage, instructs us on how to enjoy our marriage dinner by telling every bachelor and bachelorette to wait until they are actually hungry and then to eat only as much as their bodies need.

Sadly, lust makes any food taste fantastic, including junk food that is not on the marriage buffet. The marriage that God provides is nourishing and rich in the marrow, but many bachelors and bachelorettes have despised God's wonderful gifts and have a gluttonous appetite for the world's trash which is full of the meat from Egypt's fleshpots. May the Holy Spirit stir every yearning heart toward God's kind of marriage and cause them to experience the sharp pangs of marriage hunger that God has approved.

"The marriage that God provides is nourishing and rich in the marrow, but many bachelors and bachelorettes have despised God's wonderful gifts and have a gluttonous appetite for the world's trash which is full of the meat from Egypt's fleshpots."

It Is Satan's Business To Damage Holy Relationship

Satan is utterly opposed to any and all of God's blessings. He, therefore, harbors the same contempt for anyone who puts themselves in a position to benefit from such blessings. Every Christian can rest easy knowing that they will encounter Satan on the route to the holy institution of marriage at some point.

I want to humbly emphasize that every true Christian has overcome the world and its prince, Satan.

"…whatever is born of God is victorious over the world" (1 John 5:4).

However, we can all testify that we strife until death, and battle throughout life fighting with a certainty of victory. I overhear a bachelorette say:

"How and why is it that the very same gospel which usually speaks of peace declares warfare? What is going on?"

For no other reason than that there is something in the world that is hostile to love, peace, unity, sanctity, marriage, family and all of humanity. There are some principles in the world that cannot withstand light; as a result, before light can emerge and prevail, it must dispel darkness. As soon as we accept Jesus Christ as our Savior and turn into Christians, we are obligated to observe all of His commandments as His servants. Therefore, it is our responsibility to search the Bible in order to understand what Jesus said and did. Jesus Christ taught His disciples a lot through words, but He taught them considerably more through actions.

His entire life was a heavenly discourse on divine truth, and the miracles He performed served as both examples of His teaching and demonstrations of His divinity. He was constantly preaching. His miracles of mercy were actually acted sermons, physically present truths, and visually appealing demonstrations that plainly communicated the gospel message more effectively than voice speech ever could.

Christians should interpret what He did in the past to human bodies as a foreshadowing of what He will do to human souls now. Jesus is able to perform miracles in the spiritual world that are similar to those he performed in the physical world. The world's ruler governs according to a comprehensive, lengthy set of customs. People tend to swim with the flow like a dead fish, but a living fish will constantly swim against it. Thus, a true Christian who does not choose to follow world fashion is subject to social repression.

Most true Christians are well-versed in what I am saying. At some point, every Christian bachelor and bachelorette will come under attack, influence, or seduction from Satan.

Because Satan cannot be everywhere at once, he has also used his servants to carry out his evil deeds. They are some former angels who fell with him and have become demons. Satan uses these inferior spirits as his tools to seduce, attack, and ruin marriages.

In the evil business, Satan deftly utilizes commonplace occurrences and individuals. Satan does this to allow a single person - a bachelor, a bachelorette, a spouse, or a wife - to violate God's established rules in order to spread His prohibition against marriage and defamation of marriage through seemingly neutral actions.

Even though a bachelor or a bachelorette couldn't see Satan's face when they went to the movies, he was the whisperer who urged the two should cuddle up to each other. It was Satan who personally suggested to a bachelor and a bachelorette who were about to marry that they may continue having sex because it wouldn't matter because they would be getting married eventually.

Despite the fact that no one can see him, Satan is the antagonist who usually uses a trustworthy person to obstruct a planned marriage between a bachelor and a bachelorette.

Satan's actions are not the fruit of a fairy tale, a dream, or a superstitious person's imagination. He is a real person just like us. There are those whose fiercest trials from Satan come at the beginning of their marriage journey when they are bachelors and bachelorettes. There are Christian bachelors and bachelorettes who have devoted themselves to adhering to God's rules about godliness and have all their life abstained from sex, waiting for God's time. However, in an effort to stopping them from getting married, Satan tempts, resists, opposes, attacks, and defames them all because he detests everything that glorifies God. Others encounter their toughest warfare in the middle of their marriage's journey.

At a period in their marriages when they may be predisposed to believing that they are safe from Satan's attacks and that their experience and expertise will be sufficient to protect them from his cunning. Others encounter Satan near the end of their lives while they are still married. Then they remember that they are not exempt because Satan can be active in marriages at any time.

Let me get back to where I started by saying those who are born again truly overcome the world. How does this happen?

"...this is the victory that conquers the world, even our faith" (1 John 5:4).

Christians do not overcome the world intellectually in any way. I am not undermining intellect since it is a very beneficial thing. Faith is a lightbulb while intellect is a lampstand. I do not despise the lampstand; I just love the lightbulb.

The Christian bachelor and bachelorette should always employ and put to use the lamp stamp - intellect. However, when it comes to actual warfare, they must fend off lusty temptation and the like; the reason is like a timber blade that cracks and breaks. However, the sword of pure Virgin metal, faith, divides the spirit from the body; it will restrain their propensity to giving in to sexual impulses.

The Christian bachelor and bachelorette can overcome the outside world with the help of homeopathy since it uses the "like cures like" concept. We now understand how Satan opposes God and His lovely institution of marriage and how he labors ceaselessly to resist, harass, and bring about the apostasy of many marriages. And because Satan is constantly looking for methods to bring shame on God's name and His children, every Christian, especially bachelors, and bachelorettes, needs to be more vigilant and cautious.

In order to honor God and marriage, we have our lives and marriage lives propagate knowledge about love, virginity, and sanctity throughout the world. Now, even if it is a natural faith, those who have it are the ones who act in the world. Soldiers that are competent and confident to prevail in warfare are more likely to do so. Unfortunately, those who are constantly scared to take action out of worry that they will not succeed are the ones who mostly never succeed in life.

I beseech God to give every Christian, especially bachelors and bachelorettes, a brazen forehead and a daring countenance. I pray they will be people who shall have never flinched or shaken. Instead, they lifted their eyes to the hills from which their Strength emanated and decided that they would live happily ever after marriage no matter what.

"Say to the righteous that it shall be well with them, for they shall eat the fruit of their deeds". (Isaiah 3:10).

A Consecrated Bachelor Or Bachelorette Is An Overcomer

The strongest man who has ever lived or will live in the future is not Mohamed Ali, Leonid Taranenko, or Azumah Nelson but a consecrated person. Even if a person or a group of consecrate themselves to the wrong thing, if they do so thoroughly, they will still be strong - possibly Strength for evil, but it is still Strength.

Being a child of God makes every Christian a consecrated person. Jesus has not made our consecration to be characterized by any visible symbol, but He commands us to refrain from all sorts of evilness. Jesus does not command the bachelor and the bachelorette to let their hair grow out indefinitely or to not eat meat or consume alcohol. However, He forbids them from engaging in sexual activity or anything that would lead to it prior to marriage.

A bachelor and a bachelorette, as consecrated Christians, should be ambitious to make the name of God the noblest word in human language; and consequently, they will become a blessing. They have two purposes within themselves: to please the Lord with their bodies and future spouse. They should have their whole soul absorbed by those two purposes. A bachelor and a bachelorette who are everything at once and *nothing* for long, have *nothing* to live for, and are soulless corpses who wander the earth and waste its air and space. A bachelor and bachelorette who are aware of their identity, strengths, and purpose, stay focused.

Nothing can sway them from their intended course. And the basic assertion still remains true if I limit the description to what distinguishes Christian bachelors and bachelorettes - consecration to God in their virginity and to whom they give it as a gift! What bravery and dignity such a committed Christian exhibit! Many Christians, whether young or old, have privately consecrated their life to God and may say in their hearts:

"Until I am married, and the customary rites are paid, I am Jesus Christ's Bride, and He is my Bridegroom. He draws me, and I joyfully respond to His divine voice."

No matter who or what they go through, the bachelor or bachelorette who can say that and is wholly connected to God is a strong person who God, in the end, will glorify.

Remain Strong In Your Singlehood

Human *strength* comes in many different forms and varieties, and different types of *strength* are present in varying degrees in each individual. But all forms of *strength* eventually exhaust themselves, regardless of the kind the person possesses. Bodily strength is highly desired. What a blessing it is to be able to move around and be healthy, strong, and active! God can give people with incredible physical strength like Azuma Nelson, Mohamed Ali, and others. On December 1st, 1995, Ghana's Azumah Nelson defeated world champion Gabriel Rueles in the fifth round to claim the super-featherweight. Following news of Azumah's heroic deed, Ghanaians lined the streets and crowded their windows to welcome him as he rode in a vehicle through the city of Accra, Ghana, West Africa. Even though many of such people were as strong as an elephant and a leopard put together when they were young, they would inevitably become frail as they grew older.

Mental strength, often known as the power of the mind, is a superior strength that is undoubtedly much sought for. Every time we read the writings of a famous writer, we instinctively turn to the cover page to find their image. However, intelligent men have resorted to foolishness that is only fit for the dumbest. Broad knowledge has occasionally been combined with the most contemptible ambitions.

And some whose intellect appeared to be on par with that of angels have almost demonic intentions. It is unfortunate that this is the case, but a mental force devoid of morality has evolved into a destructive force and a tool for evil.

I overhear a bachelor and a bachelorette discuss where they can get the Strength to consecrate themselves to God till marriage is blessed. Without God, every bachelor or bachelorette is a prey to Satan. This is the essence of their power: as long as they are consecrated, they ought to be strong. If a bachelor and a bachelorette are completely devoted to God and have no other goal than to serve God, God will be with them and help them as long as they refrain from having sex.

"And I will strengthen [Israel] in the Lord, and they shall walk up and down and glory in His name, says the Lord" (Zachariah 10:12).

But what exactly is that strength? What sort of strength does God offer to the bachelor and the bachelorette? It is a strength that is obviously, and directly from God, and insofar as it is transferrable to the bachelor and the bachelorette, it transmits to the two a piece of the strength with which God Himself is strong in spirit. It is a strength that is so pure, so heavenly, and so divine that if the bachelor and the bachelorette are strengthened, they become spiritual Samsons. The strength expands their intellect, making them spiritual Solomon and Salome.

The strength of God enables the bachelor and the bachelorette to exert influence over others and lead like David. They are strengthened by God to be determined, loving, and devoted to accomplishing what is good so that no desire can sway them from their route or their objective. The two become morally stable strength because of God's Strength; therefore, they defend virtue even when no one is looking.

Some bachelors and bachelorettes exhibit extraordinary patience due to their supernatural Strength. Satan tests them mercilessly, but they are unconquered. Despite his efforts to destroy them, they persist: Although Satan causes them anguish, they do not give up hope. A bachelor or a bachelorette who receives strength from God Himself will be powerful in their prayer. The heaven's doors' bars start to move as they go to their knees, praying to God for mercy. Such a bachelor and a bachelorette can throw the covenant angels by wrapping their arms around his thigh. They will fight with him nonstop while exclaiming:

"And Jacob was left alone, and a Man wrestled with him until daybreak." (Genesis 32:24).

When, thus, strengthened, a bachelor and a bachelorette can conquer heaven by prayer, no matter how long it takes. With such a resolve, they can confront, with the same bravery as Elijah did when he confronted a wavering Israel on Mount Carmel, their fellow humans who question their fidelity. Such persons wield influence over their fellow humans because they interact with them as though they are well vested with supernatural power. God's Strength helps us in all aspects of our lives, including our work and life battles.

The Christian bachelor and bachelorette, who God strengthens, courageously fight their spiritual warfare not against flesh and blood but against spiritual wickedness; they do not use iron and fire but rather love and truth. While waiting to get married, the bachelor and the bachelorette who are strong in God learn to remain quiet and composed. Despite the potential delay in their marriage, they are not concerned about bad omens because their '*…heart is fixed, O God, my heart is steadfast and confident!*" - (Psalm 57:7).

Their freedom from anxiety and weakness is found in the serenity of God's power. Such a bachelor and a bachelorette are not surprised when they are tormented on all sides since they are conscious that they will have to deal with their fair share of suffering. They submit to His will regardless of how long God has instructed them to wait.

By God's grace, they can submit to everything He has ordained. Such bachelors and bachelorettes believe God is with them, and as a result, their strength is equivalent to their sorrows. They firmly trust that the all-sufficient God will meet all of their needs in accordance with His riches in glory through the person of Jesus Christ.

"And my God will liberally supply fill to the full) your every need according to His riches in glory in Christ Jesus" (Philippians 4: 19).

So, they go peacefully through this valley of sorrow. In a variety of circumstances, the power of God is tremendously beneficial. It has been wonderful for me, and I believe it will be for every Christian. Our weakness causes half of humanity's worry and disagreements. A healthy person is much less likely to dispute with anyone or feel dissatisfied with themselves than someone who is ill or weak.

May God, who is infinitely holy, unquestionably just, and immeasurably good and in whom righteousness and integrity are the cornerstones of His kingdom, grant every Christian strength for their daily walk at home and abroad, especially bachelors and bachelorettes, as this will be to the comfort of all humanity. Oh, that every Christian bachelor and bachelorette would fully embrace God's path of gaining strength!

CHAPTER 11

MARRIAGE IS A CELEBRATION OF THE BRIDE AND THE GROOM

The Bible records the various ordinances the Israelites practiced in the Tabernacles: Solomon's Temple, Zerubbabel's Temple, and Herod's Temple. God assigned the kohanim (priests) to perform the service. Sacrifices are often mentioned in the Bible (particularly in Leviticus), and the Bible devotes substantial sections to discussing the laws of the Kohanim. The Israelites made sacrifices of animals, grain, oil, wine, and other things on the altar as a vital element of their worship in the Mishkan (Tabernacle) in the desert and later in the Holy Temple in Jerusalem.

Once the Holy Temple was constructed, God prohibited the Israelites from offering sacrifices anyplace else rather than the Temple Mount in Jerusalem. God's prohibition still stands today, effectively prohibiting sacrifices anyplace other than the temple.

"And the Lord said to Moses. Tell Aaron, his sons, and all the Israelites, This is what the Lord has commanded: If any man of the house of Israel kills an ox or lamb or goat in the camp or kills it outside the camp. And does not bring it to the door of the Tent of Meeting to offer it as an offering to the Lord before the Lord's tabernacle, [guilt for shedding] blood shall be imputed to that man; he has shed blood and shall be cut off from among his people. This is so that the Israelites, rather than offer their sacrifices [to idols] in the open field [where they

slew them], may bring them to the Lord at the door of the Tent of Meeting, to the priest, to offer them as peace offerings to the Lord. And the priest shall dash the blood on the altar of the Lord at the door of the Tent of Meeting and burn the fat for a sweet and satisfying fragrance to the Lord. So they shall no more offer their sacrifices to goatlike gods or demons or field spirits after which they have played the harlot. This shall be a statute forever to them throughout their generations. And you shall say to them, Whoever of the house of Israel or of the strangers who dwell temporarily among you offers a burnt offering or sacrifice. And does not bring it to the door of the Tent of Meeting to offer it to the Lord shall be cut off from among his people" (Leviticus 17:1–9).

Every Christian, especially married couples and bachelors and bachelorettes aspiring to marry, should be familiar with every detail of Jesus Christ's death: Every insult, every slap, every disrespect, and every torment has a lesson to be learned; the sponge, the vinegar, the hyssop, and the spear that the soldier used to pierce His side; all have a purpose and are packed with knowledge.

God has instituted an ordinance for us. He has given us the Lord's Supper just as He provided the Passover to the Jewish people:

"For every time you eat this bread and drink this cup, you are representing and signifying and proclaiming the fact of the Lord's death until He comes [again]" (1 Corinthians 11:26).

God gives Christians the opportunity to experience Jesus' burial through baptism which helps in our ability to communing spiritually with Him. Therefore, the Lord's Supper or Communion is not an onerous celebration but rather a joyful one. The Lord's Supper is a happy celebration, festivity, and occasion.

Christians can perceive those two ordinances' solemnity, love, and joy when they view the Lord's Supper as a celebration and a commemoration of Jesus, the bridegroom, and the church, His bride, much as a marriage is a celebration of a bridegroom and his bride. The Passover rules and the proper observance of that sacred festival were clear and explicit, and breaking them would have been a grave offense to the God of Israel.

According to those regulations, everyone who consumed the Paschal lamb had to be ceremonially clean, and those who weren't were prohibited from partaking. As a result, they could not present the Lord's offering at the proper time.

In order to maintain the integrity of the feast, the sacred ceremony was not to be observed in mindless formality but, rather, with careful purification of the previous leaven. Jesus Christ has called us His friends by dying on the cross. Just as a bridegroom and bride welcome relatives and friends to sit and feast with them on their wedding day, Jesus has honored us by inviting us to be His table companions. While we partake in the feast with Jesus, we have a sense of being under grace rather than the law.

VENUE FOR THE CELEBRATION OF THE MARRIAGE CEREMONY

I want to start by clarifying that, strictly speaking, the location and the time of the Lord's Supper ordinance are irrelevant. No biblical passage suggests that the Lord's Supper ordinance can only be properly observed in particular times or locations, such as the morning, the afternoon, nightfall, or even in churches. The ordinance is equally effective and useful in a family's private apartments, bedrooms, or living rooms as it is in church and anywhere where Christians regularly meet.

The evening of the day is the only moment that is more like the first occasion when Jesus Christ celebrated the ordinance with His disciples. There, just prior to His crucifixion, He gathered His twelve apostles and instituted the glorious memorial feast. He also made Himself known to His two disciples at Emmaus by breaking bread at the close of the day.

The Lord's Supper is not subject to strict regulations like the Passover ordinances which are favored pleasure that is required of us by the merciful authority of the one we address as our Master and Lord. We happily accept them and are delighted. Although there is a huge reward for following those commandments, they are not presented to us as subjects of service. We accept them with joy and delight. In keeping those commandments, there is a great reward; but they are not presented to us as matters of servitude.

Having said that, I want to say also that it is said that: *"Order is the first law of heaven"*.

While some may disagree with that idea and demand biblical proof, I want to point to the Order that permeates all of God's creation as proof. Except for the human race which seems to have lost its originality of orderliness ever since Adam and Eve fell, everything that God created, from the majestic spheres that each travels in their own orbit to the tiny locus, is in perfect harmony.

"The locusts have no king, yet they go forth all of them by bands" (Proverbs 30:27).

The Christian Church is, thus, organized under God's ideals:

"Similarly when supper was ended, He took the cup also, saying, This cup is the new covenant [ratified and established] in My blood. Do this, as often as you drink [it], to call Me [affectionately] to remembrance" (1 Corinthians 11:25).

In human history, worldliness has been a demonic force that has strangled countless souls. In order to prevent its members from perishing due to such worldliness, the Christian church puts rules in place to remind Christians that we are not left without authority and guidance. Wherever there is an ordinance, there is an obligation; for there is a Law that governs everything. Things are designed to behave in a specific way, not any other way. Thus, under specific circumstances in the church's world, although it is not a universal law, many Christian churches prefer that because of the solemnization of marriage and its ordinance much like how we observe the Lord's Supper at church. We learn that the Lord's Supper should begin with thanksgiving. So, Jesus Christ Himself evidently commenced it:

"...He took a loaf [of bread], and when He had given thanks" (Luke 22:19).

Following the feast, Jesus Christ broke the bread. He offered the bread to His followers after breaking it and said: "Take, eat" and they all participated in eating it. That being done, Jesus Christ "After the same manner also He took the cup;" That is, praise God in the same way that you would express gratitude to Him for any other blessings. Throughout the supper, gratitude should be expressed in active exercise. When it was time to drink the vine's fruit from the cup, Jesus Christ said specifically, "Drink ye all of it."

The proper observance of the Lord's Supper depends on how Jesus administered it. Let us assume a priest, instead of bread, brought Macaroni and cheese and Ovaltine beverages to celebrate the Lord's Supper. He then takes the Macaroni, which isn't bread and which he doesn't break, but he took and put on a dish with a spoon and ate it all by himself. Any true Christian does not need a Super

Being to tell them that whatever the priest may choose to call his actions, it is not the Lord's Supper.

In observing the Lord's Supper, there must be a breaking of bread and a drinking of wine. Additionally, the ordinance that the Lord established must be observed by as many obedient, godly disciples of Jesus Christ as may be in the present. Even so, Christians should observe the marriage ordinance.

It is to be in the church and officiated by a priest or a designated officer of the church alongside the preaching of the Word of God, just as the Lord's Supper. As an ordinance, marriage should not be observed in a bedroom, though a bride and the groom can choose to have it done that way. However, preferably, the church wants the marriage ordinance to be observed in the presence of the congregation by an officiating minister at the church. The church has nothing against a marriage being observed at church, in a garden, at the beach, on the mountain, etc. But to prevent the liberty that grace has granted Christians from turning into a license, it prefers that a solemn ordinance like marriage be blessed and observed in the church. A priest must always preside over a marriage ceremony, witnessing the consent and granting their blessing on behalf of God.

There is a solemnity to the place where Christians gather to worship God. Many buildings, including theaters and sports arenas like the Compaq Center, were formerly used for activities other than church activity. However, as soon as Christians started to serve and worship God there, both God and society began to regard the structure as sacrosanct. Therefore, it is appropriate to say that a marriage ordinance that has been internally examined and approved by God obtains a succession of sacredness when it is externally officiated at the Church of God. God appoints a priest to serve as His spokesperson and officially declare the blessing He has already privately given to the bride and husband during the marriage ordinance. More than anything else, a newlywed couple needs to be blessed, and God has decreed that the priest should perform that blessing. Jesus Christ's public ministry officially began with the Sermon on the Mount and the expression "Blessed".

A priest declares the "Grace" of God in the blessing during a marriage ceremony. Greek speakers who are fluent in the language tell us that the term "Grace", Charis, has the word "joy" as its foundation. At the core of Grace or Charis is joy. It also stands for kindness, favor, and, most importantly, love. The secret, enigmatic seed of everything is, as it always has been, the love of God, the Father.

The priest's declaration of God's grace on behalf of God at a marriage ceremony held in a church leads to continuous communion of grace between a husband and a wife. The two hearts that God's grace pours into unite into one in appreciation. When the actual grace of God is at work in a marriage, it transforms weaknesses into strengths, anger into patience, wrongdoings into forgiveness, and hatred into love.

Therefore, the love that grace produces in a husband and a wife is compassion; it is love in its active form, loving continually sacrificing, loving safeguarding, loving enduring, loving enduring and listening, and loving honoring. The entire lives of the husband and the wife will be filled with blessings.

The Indispensable Guest

Jesus Christ did not begin the gospel epoch with a miracle of revenge even against Satan whose work He truly knows about:

"...For this purpose the Son of God was manifested, that He might destroy the works of the devil" (1 John 3:8).

The first miracle He performed was turning water into wine at the marriage ceremony in Cana of Galilee. And just as we can often tell a person's journey by its commencement, and the first step is usually the key to everything that follows, so, too, can we understand the full scope of Jesus' miracles throughout the Bible. His self-denial facilitated the miraculous marriage that unfolded. He had just returned from the wilderness and was hungry after forty days of fasting.

Whiles in the wilderness, Satan tempted Jesus Christ to turn stones into bread. Jesus had the power to order the stones to change into bread, and if He had done so, the miracle would have marked the start of signs; however, it would be a miracle He had performed for His own needs. However, such a commencement would not have been consistent with Jesus' life course, and it would have been particularly distant from His death when people said of Him:

"He saved others; Himself He cannot save. If He is the King of Israel, let Him now come down from the cross, and we will believe Him" (Matthew 27:42 NKJV).

Jesus Christ turned water into wine for others but did not turn the stones into bread for Himself. Additionally, the miracle was rendered all the more amazing by the fact that Jesus produced wine and not bread. He did not just provide bread for people, which is a basic need; instead, He went one step further and provided wine for them, which is a pleasure, despite the fact that He would not even produce bread for Himself.

The contrast between Jesus Christ's decision to deny Himself of even a crust of bread and His willingness to give to humanity - not just what might be necessary for our survival but also what was merely necessary for our joy and pleasure - is obvious and stark. When the wine ran out during the marriage ceremony, the only real risk was that the bride and groom would suffer humiliation and have their marriage undermined. However, the Triune God always endeavors to avoid the dishonoring of marriage.

Jesus Christ's presence at the marriage ceremony prevented the dignified celebration of two lovers, to which they had graciously invited Him and their families, friends, and neighbors, from collapsing by offering a resolution. Jesus, who possesses creative brilliance, thereby reciprocated the bride and groom's hospitality by bestowing a spontaneous blessing upon them.

"This also cometh forth from the Lord of hosts, which is wonderful in counsel, and excellent in working." (Isaiah 28:29).

Jesus Christ's turning of water into wine at the marriage was essential for the fulfillment of His singular purpose for marriage.

"Let marriage be held in honor (esteemed worthy, precious, of great price, and especially dear) in all things" (Hebrews 13:4).

God's profound and unfathomable blessing at the celebration of their marriage is very and always advantageous to the bride and groom. The favorable impact is felt in various ways and has a sacred effect on the husband and the wife and everyone related to them. However, I feel compelled to point out that whenever Jesus Christ is going to grant a blessing or perform a miracle, He issues a command. Everyone, especially the bride and groom, can depend on their memories to understand this fact in relation to the marriage ordinance and all other ordinances.

Although this is not always the case, a word of command generally comes before or follows a word of power. Jesus did not just say: "Let there be wine" when He was going to perform the miracle of wine to the guests and hosts at the wedding ceremony. Instead, He issued a command to the servers saying: *"...Fill the waterpots with water..." (John 2:7)*

The same is true when a priest and church officials counsel a bachelor and a bachelorette. God intends for every bride and groom to be blessed and make blessings to others. And He accomplishes that by giving them a directive through the priests and church elders. Undoubtedly, a Christian bachelor and bachelorette who plan to get married prays to God for Him to reveal His presence. The way for God to bestow His blessings on a bachelor and a bachelorette is through His command.

If a bride and a groom are to have the blessing of marriage ordinance multiplied, and many other life blessings that God bestows on a husband and a wife, they must receive the blessing from Jesus Christ because it is entirely His gift just as it was His to turn the water into wine. Yet, first of all, Jesus says to the couple:

"Adhere to all the marriage ordinances to the latter". By adhering to the marriage ordinance, the bride and groom can fill the waterpots with water. If they follow Jesus' instructions, they will experience His mighty actions as He manifests His presence at the marriage ceremony.

Every Christian, I am sure, knows that Jesus Christ is no longer physically present in His church.

Jesus Christ, who took on human nature when He was on the earth and mirrored us in every way, was physically unable to be in two places at once. He, whose humanity was similar to ours, could only be in one location at a time, just as our physical humanity is confined to being present in only one place at a time.

Jesus Christ, after completing all that the Father had given Him to do on earth, ascended to heaven bearing humanity to His home. He is now seated at the right hand of God:

"…from that time waiting till His enemies are made His footstool" (Hebrews 10:13 NKJV).

"He is not here; He has risen, as He said [He would do]. Come, see the place where He lay" (Matthew 28:6).

Jesus Christ is not physically present in His church, but the Holy Spirit acts as His representative. Jesus Christ's current emissary in the church is the Holy Spirit who is also present when a marriage is performed there. Jesus Christ will always be present at marriages and will remain so throughout the marriage ordinance because of the strength and activity of the Holy Spirit.

Just as He was physically there at Cana, Jesus Christ is present through the Holy Spirit at a marriage ceremony. The presence of Jesus Christ is made known in the marriage for all of its existence through the work of the Holy Spirit of God.

Thus, a bride and groom who observe the rules of marriage should look forward to Jesus Christ's presence through the Holy Spirit: in addition to having the Holy Ghost as the force of Jesus Christ's representation throughout their marriage ceremony, they also enjoy the divine spiritual presence of the second person of the glorious Trinity.

Every marriage that God has ordained and approved will be glorified by that presence - not a physical presence, but a spiritual presence. Any marriage without the presence of the Spirit of God may appear to be alive, but it is actually dead, and following death, comes corruption which promotes maggots in the grave of the marriage. Hence, many marriages that have strayed unto wrong paths have not only lost any ability to accomplish good but have also grown obnoxious and become major sources of evil in society.

Every Christian bachelor and bachelorette must keep in mind that they will need the Holy Spirit more than ever during their courtship and marriage preparation, as well as at their marriage ceremony and beyond. After the wedding ceremony, the husband and wife should welcome the Holy Spirit into their home as a companion because His presence suggests the life of Jesus in their home.

The bride and the groom should not only extend an invitation to the Holy Spirit to attend the marriage ceremony. They must hold Him, take His hand, pull at His pants, and bring the Well-Beloved into the most private chamber of their marriage where He will live forever with them.

After their honeymoon, the couple should not let Holy Spirit leave and should not let the nighttime chill of their marriage cast them as simpletons. And neither the bride nor the groom should permit the Holy Spirit to move a single step further away from their marriage.

Miracles At The Marriage Ceremony

Jesus Christ's mission is one of joy; thus, it begins at a marriage feast. It commences with a noble generosity deed since its goal is to impart everlasting joy and gladness to burdened hearts. The purpose of each of Jesus Christ's miracles was to fulfill a specific need.

After Adam and Eve were driven from the Garden of Eden, marriage was the last piece of heaven that remained among men. Jesus proceeded to perform His first miracle in order to glorify marriage. Marriage is according to His Father's ordinance because it was He who married Eve to Adam. So, with His Father and the Holy Spirit, Jesus Christ, Our Lord carried out His work to glorify the ordinance. He approved the ordinance that ensures the survival of the race by metaphorically touching the very sources of the human-hood.

In order to know that our marriage and family life are in His capable hands, Jesus attended the marriage ceremony and gave His blessing there. It is a miracle that confirms marriage as an institution that brings happiness, love, loyalty, and understanding to the human race through recognizing its solemnity and honor.

When the wine ran out at the wedding feast, Jesus Christ arrived just in time to save the occasion and save the bride and groom from embarrassment. Jesus had to give that circumstance at the wedding a powerful and speedy blessing to make things better. If there had been enough wine for the feast, they would never have tasted that best and purest wine, and Jesus would not have worked that miracle.

The marriage ordinance meets many blessed needs which open the door for Jesus Christ to do miraculous acts of love. No matter how kind, patient, and tolerant a husband and a wife are, life circumstances can cause them to run out of those qualities that support marriage. When a husband and a wife are in need, the Holy Spirit leads them to Jesus because He will more than supply their needs when they run out. Jesus Christ did not perform His first miracle on Jerusalem's holy sites or any other well-known cities in Palestine. However, He traveled to Galilee of the Gentiles, a region that was much hated, and it was there that Jesus performed His first miracle at the Galilean city of reeds and batons, Cana.

He did not work the sign during a grand spiritual crusade where the goal was to win souls for the heavenly kingdom. Jesus did not perform His first miracle in front of priests or scientists either. Jesus' first miracle didn't take place during a prayer group or a Bible reading; instead, it occurred at the marriage of two unnamed, poor folk. Jesus Christ shows courtesy to everyday occurrences and bestows blessings on humanity's earthly pursuits!

The miracles were incredibly generous. Jesus Christ did not multiply the bread or cake at the marriage ceremony; instead, He dealt with pleasure and filled the hearts of the bride and the groom with something as pure as the grape's bipod.

When Jesus Christ visits a marriage, He enhances the bride and groom's existing life. That life enhancement makes the bride and the groom more comfortable. God infuses His life into the marriage through the power of the Holy Spirit. He comes and breathes God's breath on the marriage ordinance at the marriage ceremony.

God is the only thing that is eternal, and the only thing that has eternal life is that which derives from Him. God's gift of marriage is not only a gift that He offers; God is also the gift that is given. He is the one who gives the marriage eternal life, which is actually Jesus Christ living within the marriage. A life that never terminates is eternal life. God's Immortal Life makes the marriage eternal; therefore, the marriage cannot come to an end.

Jesus does not only provide for a bride and a groom's marriage life and basic needs; rather, He also provides for their enjoyment which is of a higher kind. Just as He did at Cana when He changed water into wine, Jesus converts good, healthy water into a better, richer, more nutritious drink that is God-made for the bride and groom and everyone in attendance to drink. He bestows an unfathomable and glorious joy upon the bride and groom. He grants them enough grace for them to partake of "wines on the lees well refined", Jesus Christ bestows grace upon a bride and groom that they may sing, rejoice, be certain, and be filled to overflowing joy.

Jesus Christ invites a husband and a wife to a home where there is a meal of bread and wine. It is amazing that the benefactor simply requests a very modest, a simple, and a reasonable gesture from the bride and the groom in order to receive all of those blessings:

"As long as it does not violate my written Word, pay attention to everything the instructions my priest is providing you regarding the marriage ordinance."

The loyalty of a bride and a groom to God's Word is like the servants at the marriage ceremony at Cana filling up large waterpots. When Jesus wants to bless a bride and a groom during a marriage ceremony, He does not approach them with strict requirements or demands.

A Christian bachelor and a bachelorette should follow the marriage ordinance by faith in the same way that they trusted in Jesus Christ and were saved. The church's observances that adhere to the Bible's principles are perfect. It is God's word. All of those ordinances represent God's will and the will of God in action. The bride and the groom only need to adhere to the rules.

As I have repeatedly mentioned, marriage is a solemn ordinance that God instituted for humanity. Therefore, everything about it has to be solemn. The lack of understanding of the divine ordinances by humanity is a broad topic; therefore, I would not try to delve too deeply into it; instead, I will stop with the marriage ordinance. There are many things about Christianity that God does and asks us to do that we cannot understand now and probably never shall. No one can ever understand why God did not prevent Satan from deceiving Eve, resulting in an unending evil. Our highest wisdom is to be ignorant where God has not enlightened us. Anyone who acts as though they know something when they do not becomes greatly frustrated.

No human being who comes close to understanding the terrifying mystery of God's Providence has ever lived or will ever live. Let's let God's "Whys" and "Whats" alone so that we do not lose sight of our reason.

Jesus once humbled Himself by adding water to a bowl and washing His disciples' feet while He was present with them. It was really simple and obviously a very kind, considerate, and courteous gesture. Peter, however, obviously thought that Jesus' action was highly mysterious. He, thus, resisted. Jesus Christ responded to this opposition by saying:

"…You do not understand now what I am doing, but you will understand later on" (John 13:6).

The same expression: *"What I do you know not"*, can be used to describe the Christian church's marriage ordinances which many Christians have observed for generations.

Human beings are unable to understand the finer details of how God bestows His blessing. Whether or not Peter understood what Jesus was doing when He washed his feet, Jesus washed them thoroughly regardless.

We might not be familiar with the chemical components of our doctors' medications for our illnesses. But because medicine has properties rather than being dependent on a patient's understanding, when we take the drug, it cures our illnesses.

An ignorant person will be satisfied by Rice and Fish just as a physician who knows how the body absorbs food. We all are not Sir Isaac Newton, for we are ignorant of the laws of light, yet we can see. Most of us are quick to hear sounds despite having little or no knowledge of Physics. Many people are completely ignorant of aviation and all of its components. Despite this, we flew from far and wide as though we had gone to a pilot training.

By limiting myself to God's blessings on the church's marriage ordinance, it is safe to assume that no human can predict with certainty the exact course of God's blessings for a bride and a groom. Many brides and grooms forfeit the richest blessings of marriage for want of clear perception.

What could be a greater consolation to the passionate bachelor and the bachelorette than to know that their well Beloved will be present at their marriage ceremony and to watch Him manifestly appear to turn water into wine? I draw the attention of every prospective bride and groom with these words:

"By faith Abraham, when he was called, obeyed..." (Hebrews 11:8).

What a blessing it would be if the Holy Spirit taught us all how to obey!

If a bride and a groom were complete in their obedience in everything pertaining to their Christian life and marriage, how fully should they be blessed?

What a heaven there would be on earth if everyone obeyed Jesus Christ!

Perfect obedience to God would entail love for husband and wife, families, churches, and nations. Such obedience will result in peace throughout the world and justice for all social strata. Sadly, although Jesus' "Will" provides us peace, delight, love, and joy, human "Will" only brings jealousy, hatred, and conflict.

*"Our highest wisdom is to be ignorant where
God has not enlightened us. Anyone who
acts as though they know something
when they do not becomes greatly frustrated."*

PROSPECTIVE COUPLES MUST STAY OUT OF FORNICATION

Children are supposed to resemble their parents in some way. Children of God, who are the greatest of all parents and are renewed by the overwhelming power of the Holy Spirit, are certain to resemble their heavenly Father to a great extent.

It is impossible for us to exercise His power or to have His unlimited knowledge, nor can we be independent and self-existent or possessors of sovereignty or worshipfulness because those qualities belong to God alone and are not transferable. Jesus is the only begotten Son of God in a mystical manner; no man can ever be more clearly the image of the Father.

But we might emulate many aspects of God, especially those that are moral and spiritual. Without those characteristics, it is impossible to decipher our heavenly ancestry.

"Therefore be imitators of God [copy Him and follow His example], as well-beloved children [imitate their father]" (Ephesians 5:1).

God assigned Apostle Paul the duty of reminding His people of His counsel by mentioning the One to Whom he had dedicated His love and the purity of His flesh.

"Do you not know that the unrighteous and the wrongdoers will not inherit or have any share in the kingdom of God? Do not be deceived (misled): neither the impure and immoral, nor idolaters, nor adulterers, nor those who participate in homosexuality" (1 Corinthians 6:9).

Fornicators, or men and women who have engaged in unchaste acts with unmarried people, are the first kind of sinners described in Paul's horrifying list. Christians must always be bound to one another in the bonds of purity as well as the bonds of matrimony. People who breach purity rules in their interactions with one another are not eligible for God's kingdom. God would not permit anyone who engages in lust and sexual immorality to profane His heavenly temple or defile His true Church on earth.

There cannot be a misunderstanding about the plain fact that no one can be a Christian if they defile themselves in fornication. They cannot be God's children and live in filthy sin as fornication.

Through the apostle Paul, God excommunicated everyone who fraudulently claimed to be a member of His Church while engaging in immorality because it must not be - it cannot be.

Every Christian's body is the temple of the Holy Ghost for all purposes and intents.

"Do you not know that your body is the temple (the very sanctuary) of the Holy Spirit Who lives within you, Whom you have received [as a Gift] from God? You are not your own." (I Corinthians 6:19).

Since bodily immorality is a blasphemous degradation of our humanness and a violation of the hallowed sanctuary where the Holy Spirit takes up residence, we should not be profaned. Thus, Apostle Paul grabs fornication and drags it to the foot of the cross where it is nailed hand and foot to death like a criminal.

"You were bought with a price [purchased with a preciousness and paid for, made His own]. So then, honor God and bring glory to Him in your body" (1 Corinthians 6:20)

The blood of Jesus is the method by which we have been bought from fornication. If Christians are not our own but rather "are bought with a price", then we do not have the right to exercise any arbitrary self-government.

A bachelor and a bachelorette who are their own may say:
"We will have sex even though we are not married"

But a Christian bachelor and a bachelorette who know they are not their own will say:

"We do not own our bodies; therefore we cannot do what we like with it."

Christians must submit to God's governance; His will must be our desire, and His commands must be our law because we are not our own but God's possession that He has bought.

I desire to enter Buckingham Palace, and I ask the King's Guard at the gate if I may come in. Because King Charles has not instructed the Guard to let me in, he might answer:

"Mom, I wish I could let you into the Palace if I own it, but King Charles has told me not to admit strangers into the Palace, and therefore, I have no choice but to refuse you from coming in."

In the same way when Satan sends fornication to come inside of a Christian's body, we should tell him (Satan) King Jesus has not told us to allow you in; and we cannot let you in because our body, the temple, is not ours.

Let there be no mistake concerning this matter; no one can be Christians if they, thus, defile themselves; they cannot be children of God and live in filthy sin; it must not - it cannot be, and God here, by the pen of Apostle Paul, excommunicates all who pretend to be members of His church, and yet are guilty of the sin of fornication. That means such a person who is being excommunicated by God cannot get internal approval from God to marry.

Many bachelors and bachelorettes are excommunicated by God in the invisible church, but because their behavior has not been revealed, they still seem to be active in the visible church. They might proceed with blessing their external marriage, but God might not have given His inward blessing.

Therefore, it is advisable for any bachelor or bachelorette who is aware that their act of fornication has caused them to be excommunicated by God to put a stop to all plans for getting married at the church until they are reconciled with God and reinstated.

"We do not own our bodies; therefore we cannot do what we like with it."

Epilogue

Dearly Beloved Reader, I have humbly put before your mind's eye a fair picture of the Solemnity of Singlehood, Marriage, Family, Church, and the State. All of them began as a Home; a word as sweet as heaven, and a healthy, happy race of children is as fine a possession as even angels can desire. However, on the part of God, none of those should be a rock we should build our hopes on; securing as our portion the godly instructions of this book will help us cheerfully renounce the dreamy joys of religion.

God, who dwells in His church, completely frowns on the fact that we regard any of those as the chief end and the real object of our being. If it is in the "WILL" of God, we are to marry and be married.

We should strive to navigate life's difficulties and pleasures with dignity, acquire knowledge, wealth, and comfort, and finally use all the world's privileges without cruelty. We should live a very peaceful and quiet life far distant from the wasteful, immoral, indifferent, or perverted persona that will be an obstacle to others.

"Life is solemn; life is beautiful:"

It is equally solemn for all humanity thus far. Life is solemn in the gratitude we owe God for the blessings He is pleased to give us. Life is solemn for work and God's operation. It is true in the solemn humanitarian obligation it imposes on us. Life is solemn to us inasmuch as we can perceive God in it and use it to glorify Him.

The unreality of the solemnity of life to many people in the world is found in the fact that they live for only now. This is the wand that touches the substance and makes it, before the eye of wisdom, dissolve into a shade.

There is another world in view! There is nothing here in the present world but what is proper and right. Yet, everything is improper, and everything becomes wrong at once if they are thought to be the substantial things for which an immortal spirit is to spend its fires and for which an undying soul is to exhaust its powers.

"What is human? And what is marriage, wealth, fame, beauty, etc.? It is not here but gone!" To conclude at once that we come to this world alone, and naked and alone we depart with nothing, we have only to think of what life is when a husband, a wife, and children in a fatal accident are placed in different coffins at their funeral! Such a depiction at funerals is simply a little intermission in the middle of eternity's grandeur, a narrow piece of land sticking out into the great, whether delightful or woeful and unfathomable sea of everlastingness!

Acknowledgment

I am exceedingly grateful to God for making me see much benevolence in action toward me. I gratefully ascribe all glory not to my own effort but to God's grace, mercy, and goodness.

Anyone who knows me well would attest that my life is chock-full of examples of the truth David stated in the following words:

"Your gentleness and condescension have made me…" (Psalm 18:35b).

God's condescension can serve as a comprehensive interpretation of my whole life. It is God's making Himself little, which is the cause of my being able to do anything. I am so little that if God should have manifested His greatness without condescension, I should be trampled under His feet. But God, who must stoop to view the skies and bow to see what angels do, has been gracious to me to bend His eye yet lower and look to the lowly and the contrite and give me grace.

The God who does not sell grace or glory, He who does not put them up to auction to those who can give something in return for them in His robes of grace has been merciful to meet me on the ground of being a nobody and undeserving, and said to me: "I will be gracious unto you." He has given me grace without money, grace without price, and grace without any merit in me. My prayer is to continually love you, God, more than anyone and anything in the world.

Dad, who is now in heaven, you know that I would if I could give everything to maintain an unbroken and intimate fellowship with you. But alas, in this world, our bodies are subject to death, so we do not get or become what we always wish for. While on earth, you were a testimony to what God can do for her daughter through a father. Thank you, Dad, for looking beyond yourself to care for other people's welfare. Love you, Dad! But you do not have the right to be asleep for this long, for your beloved daughter misses you.

To my family: Dads, Moms, Aunts, and Siblings, you know I have a deep love for you for who you all are to me. And I express my appreciation to you all.

For their untold hours of editing and sharing of ideas, I express my heartfelt thanks to Rev. Vincent Davies. You have been a great blessing to me. Without your commitment, this book could not have been completed. To Apostle Retired Joseph Kwame Asabil (Former International Executive Council Member, Church of Pentecost), Agyei Kwarteng (International Executive Council Member, Church Of Pentecost, Area Head Bompata Kumasi), Apostle Michael Kwame Etrue (Executive Council Member, Church of Pentecost, Area Head, Koforidua, and Eastern Region Regional Coordinator), Apostle Samuel Edzii Davidson (Church of Pentecost, Offinso Area Head), Apostle George Kwaku Korankye (Church of Pentecost, United Kingdom), Pastor Kwasi Afoakwah-Duah (Church of Pentecost, Galilea District Accra), and Pastor Richard Nsiah (Church of Pentecost, New York District), Mrs. Faustina Anane-Sarfo, wife of Apostle Isaac Anane-Sarfo, New York Area Head, Church of Pentecost USA INC, I convey my heartfelt gratitude, which words are not able to express, to you. You grabbed the vision and would not let go; despite incredible deadline pressures, you read the necessary material to be able to write an endorsement for the book. Thank you for making God's vision your vision. Whenever I think about what you have done, I envision that day when we all, in a loving fellowship as a church, will come to the great gathering of God, the holy convocation of saints of every tongue, the central home of all the tribes of His great family.

Your collective contribution has well been for solemn purposes; for it is an act for joyous purposes; a solemn joy, a holy delight for the restoration of broken marriages, families, homes, and the world.

I humbly pray that God will forever remember what you have done and bless you accordingly. You have brought me joy.

I am indebted to every priest and wife of the Church of Pentecost and beyond for your godly example.

I humbly thank all ministers and wives of the Church of Pentecost, USA INC. I appreciate their indirect role in gracing every word in the book and providing advice.

I can never stop thinking of the generous advice, consolations, and encouragement that some women and men in my life rendered to me when I needed it most. You have prayed with me to advance this worthy cause. There is wisdom in many counselors. Your love, prayers, and advice are invaluable.

I am grateful to all of you who have shared your personal experiences regarding Singleness, Marriage, Family, etc. Your testimonies will not only inspire others, but they will also make this book more appealing.

They provide not only informative examples but also spectacular key points along the journey. It's mesmerizing! Thank you very much.

As I put down my pen for the last time, I humbly offer a blessing to everyone who reads this book. May the grace of our Lord Jesus Christ and the Son of God be with you. May the grace of that exceptional Person who is God and Man in one Person and who is the church's bridegroom continue to be solemnly bestowed on you. May the grace that comes with His supremacy, His kingship, and His divinely human sovereignty come to you all.

Holy Spirit, I will be forever grateful to You.

WELCOME TO OUR PARACLETE FAMILY!!

Whether you received this book as a gift, borrowed it, or purchased it yourself, we are glad you read it. It is just one of the many helpful, insightful, and encouraging resources produced by our Paraclete family.

Many Christians have long been Christians, have grown rich in experience, and known God's love and faithfulness.

Please, let us look out for the little ones, and speak to them goodly and in comfortable words, whereby they may be cheered and strengthened. When we determine the little ones have weakness, in the plentitude of our wisdom and experience, we need to advice and train them. Let's not withhold graces from them when we have no intention to help them get better and become useful to the family of God and the communities of the world.

Please, let's act in a noble and a virtuous part to cheer the little ones up and bade them of good courage. Some have been wounded not because of their faults but by the people they trusted. Therefore, let's please salute them with words of tender encouragement; for this is precisely what Christians do.

Above all else, let's cease not to pray for the little ones till their little heart is completely and forever given to God. Be a Prophet Samuel to the little ones as he was to David. Be a Naomi to the little ones, and she was to Ruth. Be Elizabeth to the little ones as she was to Mary, for you may be nurturing a king of Israel or a descendant of Jesus Christ, the Savior of the world.

In fact, that is what the Paraclete is all about - providing inspiration, comfort, advocacy, guidance, information, and godly advice to people in all stages of life.

May our Paraclete, the Third Person of the Blessed Trinity, enlighten us so that we will know that we are one family fighting a common enemy called Satan. May He bless us so that we can be a blessing to everyone that comes our way. Amen!

EMAIL US YOUR STORY!!!

Please, give us the privilege of hearing how the conversations in AS IT WAS IN THE BEGINNING have impacted you, your Single Life, your Marriage, your Family or your Loved One.

Email Ewuramma via:
ourparacletefoundation.inc@gmail.com

Our Paraclete Foundation Inc. is a non-profit organization established to bring to remembrance that everyone is the DARLING of God.

Our objective is to let every person know and feel that God loves us unconditionally so that as a natural result, we will love Him in return; and in proportion, as our love knowledge increases, our faith strengthens, and our conviction to love one another deepens, the world will know that we are really ONE FAMILY AND FROM ONE RACE.

I pray that God will grant us the grace so that the very constitution of our being will be constrained to yield our hearts to God into building godly human and marriage relationships.

Appendix

1. City upon a Hill - Wikipedia. https://en.wikipedia.org/wiki/City_upon_a_Hill

2. Dedham Pulpit: Or, Sermons by the Pastors of the First Church in Dedham in ... - Ebenezer Burgess, First Church (Dedham, Mass.) - Google Llibres. https://books.google.ad/books?pg=PA343&vq=%22O+ye+hypocrites,+ye+can+discern+the+face+of+the+sky,+but+can+ye+not+discern+the+signs+of+the%22&dq=editions:OXFORD590230206&lr=&id=hDoPAAAAIAAJ&hl=ca&output=text

3. Finishing | Jesus Speaks. https://jesusspeaks.com/tag/finishing/

4. Potential secretary of state Mitt Romney met Donald Trump at Jean Georges in Trump Tower and ate chocolate cake with Reince Priebus. https://qz.com/849010/potential-secretary-of-state-mitt-romney-met-donald-trump-at-jean-georges-in-trump-tower-and-ate-chocolate-cake-with-reince-priebus

5. Purity & Chastity Â–Heir Force Ministries. href="https://goheirforce.com/library/devotionals/daily-reading-plan/sacrifices-in-the-temple/purity-chastity/">https://goheirforce.com/library/devotionals/daily-reading-plan/sacrifices-in-the-temple/purity-chastity/

6. The Encapsulation Of Seed Technology (Part 2): The Expedition To The Holy Estate | INFEMI Sermon By Minister Evans Ochieng, Ân Infinite Fellowship Ministries. https://

infemi.org/2019/09/22/the-encapsulation-of-seed-technology-part-2-the-expedition-to-the-holy-estate-infemi-sermon-by-minister-evans-ochieng/

7. The election of Barack Obama. https://theologicalpipe.com/2008/11/08/the-election-of-barack-obama/

8. Trouble on the Hill | thinkinthemorning.com. https://thinkinthemorning.com/trouble-on-the-hill/

9. Why The Russia Investigation Matters And Why You Should Care. https://www.spokanepublicradio.org/2017-05-24/why-the-russia-investigation-matters-and-why-you-should-care

10. じじぃの「歴史・思想_403_2050 年 世界人口大減少・最強のアメリカ」- cool-hiraÂ's diary. < href="https://cool-hira.hatenablog.com/entry/2020/12/18/060810">https://cool-hira.hatenablog.com/entry/2020/12/18/060810

END OF VOLUME TWO

www.ingramcontent.com/pod-product-compliance
Lightning Source LLC
Chambersburg PA
CBHW071904290426
44110CB00013B/1275